Low Cholesterol Cool for Beginners

2000 + Days of Easy & Delicious Recipes to Lower Cholesterol, Improve Heart Health and Eating Well Every Day. Stress-Free 60-Day Meal Plan

Lisa Mckeith

TABLE OF CONTENTS

INTRODUCTION

What cholesterol is, and what it is used for

Cholesterol is an essential component of our body, fundamental for regulating the exchange of substances useful for the life of cells and therefore, of our body. It is, in fact, the basic substance for the formation of steroid hormones such as cortisol and aldosterone, sex hormones such as testosterone and estradiol, and vitamin D.

Cholesterol also has an important digestive function: the liver converts it into bile salts, indispensable substances for proper digestion. Partly produced by the liver and partly introduced with food, our body tends to keep it at a constant level. In the fasting phase, therefore, the liver produces the necessary quota, while after meals, the share of absorbed cholesterol inhibits the action of the liver, which is put to rest.

Cholesterol "good" and cholesterol "bad"

Cholesterol is actually only one, but the proteins that carry it in the blood change. According to them, therefore, a distinction can be made between:

LDL cholesterol (bad cholesterol) is carried by proteins that bring it into circulation from the liver to the tissues with the risk of depositing it on the arteries and forming, in the long run, dangerous lipid plaques that can obstruct normal blood circulation in the vessel

HDL cholesterol (good cholesterol), whose proteins recover cholesterol from the periphery and bring it back to the liver, where it is degraded and eliminated.

The risks associated with high cholesterol

A high level of cholesterol in the blood, especially of the LDL type, represents one of the main risk factors for cardiovascular diseases, which are the main cause of mortality in the world. In subjects with hyperlipidemia, the decrease in blood fats also leads to a linear reduction in cardiopathic risk.

Until recently, only total cholesterol was referred to. The accepted level was 250 mg/dl. Today, we evaluate bad cholesterol, that is, that transported by LDL.

Total HDL cholesterol and triglyceride measurement is normally found on blood tests, but often, LDL cholesterol does not appear. This can, however be calculated by applying a simple mathematical formula: LDL = Total cholesterol - (HDL + Triglycerides / 5).

The optimal LDL values are different according to the associated pathologies, generally from 160 to 130 mg/dl. A person with diabetes mellitus should have LDL cholesterol not exceeding 100 mg/dl, while a heart patient has a level not exceeding 70 mg/dl.

How to lower high cholesterol

Cholesterol reduction can be pursued through:

- a balanced diet without excess
- the increase in physical activity
- the abolition of smoking

- the reduction of body weight.

If the objectives are not achieved, the attending physician will have to carefully evaluate, based on the general conditions of the individual patient, the need to undertake drug therapy.

The diet to follow

Dietotherapy aims to normalize weight and decrease the cholesterol supply introduced with nutrition. The most important thing is to reduce the amount of animal fats (sausages, red meats, cheeses, eggs), which will be replaced by vegetable proteins (legumes). These nutrients are useful because they bring fibers and exercise the role of antioxidants.

It is also recommended to eat fish and meat, rich in fats that we can define as good, which exercise a protective action, especially for the cardiovascular system. However, it is good to avoid crustaceans, which are rich in cholesterol and prefer blue fish.

The amount of lipids (fat) must correspond (and, if necessary, be reduced) to about a third of the total daily caloric ration. However, it is a matter of limiting saturated fats (the " bad fats "), which favor the increase in cholesterol (in particular, c-LDL), in favor of unsaturated fats, which include omega 3s. These fatty acids are indispensable for the proper functioning of the body and can help to reduce LDL cholesterol.

The method of cooking food can also make a difference in keeping cholesterol under control. In this sense, it would be better to prefer baked or steamed cooking at low temperatures or at pressure.

What are the foods to avoid for high cholesterol?

As we have seen, it is possible to intervene in cholesterol levels to try to lower them through a healthy and balanced diet. First of all, to combat high cholesterol, limiting the supply of foods rich in saturated fatty acids and cholesterol is necessary.

Animal fats are, therefore, to be avoided, such as:

- fatty meats (pork, lamb, mutton, goose)
- salami
- offal
- butter
- cream
- whole milk
- cheeses with more than 40% fat
- egg yolk

Among the other foods to be avoided for high cholesterol, we can still mention different types of oils (peanuts, palm, coconut), in addition to lard and, in general, fried foods.

Finally, in a diet aimed at keeping cholesterol within normal levels, various croissants, desserts, industrial-ready meals, chocolate, chocolate drinks, and ice cream should not appear.

What to eat when you have high cholesterol

Not all foods are taboo to fight high cholesterol. In this sense, it is necessary to prefer white lean meats, poultry, fish, milk (skimmed or partially skimmed), yogurt, and skimmed cheeses.

We should also privilege those foods that are rich in unsaturated fats, such as extra virgin olive oil, sunflower oil, grape seeds, corn, or rapeseed.

It is also recommended to increase the intake of omega-3, a polyunsaturated fatty acid that can be found in:

- fatty fish from cold seas (mackerel, sardines, anchovies, non-farmed salmon)
- flax and rapeseed, dried fruit and nuts
- green leafy vegetables (valereianella, cabbage, lettuce)
- edible algae.

The purpose of this diet should be to maintain (or find) a balanced and varied diet rich in fruit and vegetables, including carefully chosen lipids, proteins, and carbohydrates, preferably slow-shaped (bread, cereals).

At one time, it was recommended to no longer favor sunflower or corn margarine because it has proved carcinogenic.

An example of a diet for high-cholesterol

A particularly functional feeding model not only to counteract high cholesterol levels is certainly the Mediterranean diet, declared a UNESCO World Heritage Site in 2010. This diet is based on the consumption of fresh plant-based foods, olive oil as the main source of fats, moderate dairy products, fish and white meats, and wine to the meal in moderate quantities.

Another important aspect concerns the diversification of foods, taking into account that the consumption of high cholesterol levels can be tolerated, provided that it is occasional.

The Mediterranean diet also includes snacks (lean white yogurt/fruit/fruit / wholemeal rusks) in the mid-morning and mid-afternoon for a total of five meals a day.

The following recipes are tasty and easy to develop; have fun and think about your health! Good fun!

1. Oatmeal with Blueberries and Almonds

Introduction: This heart-healthy breakfast combines the fiber-rich goodness of oats with the antioxidant power of blueberries and the crunch of almonds, making it a perfect choice for those looking to lower their cholesterol levels.

Prep Time: 5 minutes | Cook Time: 5 minutes | Yield: 2 servings

Ingredients

- 1 cup rolled oats
- 2 cups unsweetened almond milk
- 1 cup fresh blueberries
- 1/4 cup sliced almonds
- 1 tablespoon honey (optional)
- 1/2 teaspoon vanilla extract
- Pinch of salt

Method of Preparation

1. In a saucepan, combine the rolled oats and almond milk. Cook over medium heat, stirring occasionally, for about 5 minutes or until the oats are creamy and tender.
2. Stir in the vanilla extract and a pinch of salt. If desired, drizzle honey over the oatmeal for sweetness.
3. Divide the oatmeal into two bowls. Top each serving with fresh blueberries and sliced almonds.
4. Serve hot and enjoy your cholesterol-friendly breakfast!

Nutritional Facts (per serving): Calories: 280 | Total Fat: 8g | Saturated Fat: 1g | Cholesterol: 0mg | Sodium: 120mg | Carbohydrates: 47g | Dietary Fiber: 7g | Sugars: 13g | Protein: 8g

2. Avocado and Spinach Breakfast Burrito

Introduction: Start your day with a nutrient-packed breakfast burrito filled with creamy avocado, spinach, and eggs, all wrapped in a whole-grain tortilla.

Prep Time: 10 minutes | Cook Time: 10 minutes | Yield: 2 burritos

Ingredients

- 4 large eggs
- 2 whole-grain tortillas
- 1 ripe avocado, sliced
- 1 cup fresh spinach leaves
- 1/4 cup diced tomatoes
- 2 tablespoons chopped fresh cilantro
- Salt and pepper to taste
- Salsa (optional, for serving)

Method of Preparation

1. In a bowl, whisk the eggs and season with salt and pepper.
2. Heat a non-stick skillet over medium heat. Pour the whisked eggs into the skillet and cook, stirring gently, until they are just set.
3. Warm the whole-grain tortillas in a dry skillet or microwave for a few seconds.
4. Lay out each tortilla and divide the scrambled eggs evenly between them.
5. Top the eggs with sliced avocado, fresh spinach leaves, diced tomatoes, and chopped cilantro.
6. Fold the sides of the tortillas inwards, then roll them up from the bottom to create burritos.
7. Serve with salsa if desired and enjoy your cholesterol-friendly breakfast!

Nutritional Facts (per burrito): Calories: 350 | Total Fat: 21g | Saturated Fat: 4g | Cholesterol: 370mg | Sodium: 310mg | Carbohydrates: 26g | Dietary Fiber: 9g | Sugars: 2g | Protein: 15g

3. Greek Yogurt Parfait with Mixed Berries

Introduction: This Greek yogurt parfait is a delightful and nutritious way to start your day. It's packed with protein, fiber, and antioxidants from mixed berries.

Prep Time: 10 minutes | Yield: 2 servings

Ingredients:

- 1 cup Greek yogurt (low-fat or non-fat)
- 1 cup mixed berries (e.g., strawberries, blueberries, raspberries)
- 1/4 cup granola (low-sugar)
- 2 tablespoons honey (optional)

Method of Preparation:

1. In two glasses or bowls, layer the Greek yogurt, mixed berries, and granola alternately.
2. Drizzle honey on top if you prefer added sweetness.
3. Repeat the layering process until the glasses are filled.
4. Serve immediately and enjoy your cholesterol-friendly breakfast parfait!

Nutritional Facts (per serving): Calories: 220 | Total Fat: 4g | Saturated Fat: 0g | Cholesterol: 10mg | Sodium: 60mg | Carbohydrates: 35g | Dietary Fiber: 4g | Sugars: 21g | Protein: 15g

4. Spinach and Mushroom Egg White Scramble

Introduction: This egg white scramble is a low-cholesterol breakfast option filled with the goodness of spinach and mushrooms, making it a heart-healthy choice.

Prep Time: 10 minutes | Cook Time: 10 minutes | Yield: 2 servings

Ingredients

- 4 large egg whites
- 1 cup fresh spinach leaves
- 1/2 cup sliced mushrooms
- 1/4 cup diced onions
- 1 clove garlic, minced
- 2 tablespoons low-fat feta cheese (optional)
- Salt and pepper to taste
- Cooking spray

Method of Preparation

1. Heat a non-stick skillet over medium heat and lightly coat it with cooking spray.
2. Add diced onions and minced garlic to the skillet. Sauté for a few minutes until they become translucent.
3. Add sliced mushrooms and cook until they release their moisture and become tender.
4. Stir in fresh spinach leaves and cook until they wilt.
5. In a separate bowl, whisk the egg whites, salt, and pepper.
6. Pour the egg white mixture into the skillet with the cooked vegetables. Cook and gently scramble until the eggs are set.
7. If desired, sprinkle low-fat feta cheese over the top and let it melt slightly.
8. Serve hot and enjoy your cholesterol-friendly egg white scramble!

Nutritional Facts (per serving): Calories: 80 | Total Fat: 0.5g | Saturated Fat: 0g | Cholesterol: 0mg | Sodium: 210mg | Carbohydrates: 4g | Dietary Fiber: 1g | Sugars: 2g | Protein: 15g

5. Quinoa Porridge with Chia Seeds and Banana

Introduction: This hearty and cholesterol-friendly quinoa porridge is packed with protein and fiber, making it a perfect way to kick-start your day.

Prep Time: 5 minutes | Cook Time: 15 minutes | Yield: 2 servings

Ingredients:

- 1/2 cup quinoa, rinsed
- 1 cup unsweetened almond milk
- 1 ripe banana, mashed
- 2 tablespoons chia seeds
- 1/2 teaspoon ground cinnamon
- 1/4 teaspoon vanilla extract
- 1 tablespoon honey (optional)
- Sliced banana and chopped nuts for garnish

Method of Preparation:

1. In a saucepan, combine quinoa and almond milk. Bring to a boil, then reduce the heat and simmer for about 10-15 minutes, or until the quinoa is tender and most of the liquid is absorbed.
2. Stir in the mashed banana, chia seeds, ground cinnamon, and vanilla extract. Cook for an additional 2-3 minutes, stirring occasionally.
3. If desired, drizzle honey over the porridge for added sweetness.
4. Divide the quinoa porridge into two bowls and garnish with sliced banana and chopped nuts.

5. Serve warm and enjoy your cholesterol-friendly quinoa porridge!

Nutritional Facts (per serving): Calories: 300 | Total Fat: 7g | Saturated Fat: 0.5g | Cholesterol: 0mg | Sodium: 90mg | Carbohydrates: 54g | Dietary Fiber: 8g | Sugars: 15g | Protein: 7g

6. Whole Wheat Pancakes with Fresh Fruit Compote

Introduction: These whole wheat pancakes are both heart-healthy and delicious, topped with a fresh fruit compote for a burst of flavor.

Prep Time: 15 minutes | Cook Time: 15 minutes | Yield: 4 servings

Ingredients:

For Pancakes:

- 1 cup whole wheat flour
- 1 tablespoon sugar (or sweetener of choice)
- 1 teaspoon baking powder
- 1/2 teaspoon baking soda
- 1/4 teaspoon salt
- 1 cup low-fat buttermilk
- 1 large egg
- 1 tablespoon canola oil
- 1 teaspoon vanilla extract

For Fruit Compote:

- 2 cups mixed fresh fruit (e.g., berries, sliced peaches, sliced kiwi)
- 2 tablespoons honey
- 1 teaspoon lemon juice

Method of Preparation:

For Pancakes:

1. In a mixing bowl, combine whole wheat flour, sugar, baking powder, baking soda, and salt.
2. In another bowl, whisk together buttermilk, egg, canola oil, and vanilla extract.
3. Pour the wet ingredients into the dry ingredients and stir until just combined. Do not overmix; it's okay if there are lumps.
4. Heat a non-stick griddle or skillet over medium-high heat. Lightly grease with cooking spray or oil.
5. Pour 1/4 cup portions of pancake batter onto the griddle. Cook until bubbles form on the surface, then flip and cook until golden brown on both sides.

For Fruit Compote:

1. In a small saucepan, combine mixed fresh fruit, honey, and lemon juice.
2. Cook over low heat, stirring occasionally, until the fruit softens and releases juices, about 5 minutes.
3. Remove from heat and let it cool slightly.
4. Serve the whole wheat pancakes topped with the fresh fruit compote.
5. Enjoy your cholesterol-friendly whole wheat pancakes with fresh fruit compote!

Nutritional Facts (per serving, including fruit compote): Calories: 240 | Total Fat: 4g | Saturated Fat: 0.5g | Cholesterol: 40mg | Sodium: 350mg | Carbohydrates: 47g | Dietary Fiber: 6g | Sugars: 23g | Protein: 6g

7. Tofu and Vegetable Breakfast Stir-Fry

Introduction: This tofu and vegetable breakfast stir-fry is a protein-packed, cholesterol-friendly option that's both satisfying and nutritious.

Prep Time: 10 minutes | Cook Time: 15 minutes | Yield: 2 servings

Ingredients

- 8 oz firm tofu, cubed
- 1 cup mixed vegetables (e.g., bell peppers, broccoli, carrots)
- 1/4 cup diced onions
- 2 cloves garlic, minced
- 2 tablespoons low-sodium soy sauce
- 1 tablespoon sesame oil
- 1/2 teaspoon ground ginger
- 1/2 teaspoon red pepper flakes (optional)
- Salt and pepper to taste
- Cooking spray

Method of Preparation

1. Heat a non-stick skillet or wok over medium-high heat and lightly coat it with cooking spray.
2. Add diced onions and minced garlic to the skillet. Stir-fry for a minute until fragrant.
3. Add tofu cubes and cook until lightly browned on all sides.
4. Stir in mixed vegetables and continue to stir-fry for about 5-7 minutes until the vegetables are tender-crisp.
5. In a small bowl, whisk together low-sodium soy sauce, sesame oil, ground ginger, and red pepper flakes (if using).
6. Pour the sauce over the tofu and vegetables. Stir-fry for an additional 2 minutes until everything is coated evenly.
7. Season with salt and pepper to taste.
8. Serve hot and enjoy your cholesterol-friendly tofu and vegetable breakfast stir-fry!

Nutritional Facts (per serving): Calories: 220 | Total Fat: 12g | Saturated Fat: 2g | Cholesterol: 0mg | Sodium: 420mg | Carbohydrates: 16g | Dietary Fiber: 4g | Sugars: 5g | Protein: 14g

8. Sweet Potato and Kale Hash with Poached Eggs

Introduction: This sweet potato and kale hash with poached eggs is a nutrient-packed breakfast that's high in fiber and flavor, perfect for those aiming to lower cholesterol levels.

Prep Time: 15 minutes | Cook Time: 20 minutes | Yield: 2 servings

Ingredients:

- 2 medium sweet potatoes, peeled and diced
- 2 cups fresh kale, chopped
- 1/2 cup diced onions
- 2 cloves garlic, minced
- 4 large eggs
- 1 tablespoon olive oil
- Salt and pepper to taste
- Cooking spray

Method of Preparation:

1. Heat a large skillet over medium heat and add olive oil. Add diced sweet potatoes and cook for about 10-12 minutes until they are tender and slightly crispy. Stir occasionally.
2. Add diced onions and minced garlic to the skillet. Sauté for another 2 minutes until the onions are translucent.
3. Stir in chopped kale and cook for an additional 2-3 minutes until the kale is wilted and bright green. Season with salt and pepper.
4. While the hash is cooking, poach the eggs. Fill a large saucepan with water, bring it to a gentle simmer, and add a splash of vinegar. Crack each egg into a small bowl, then gently slide them into the simmering water. Poach for 3-4 minutes for runny

yolks or longer if desired. Remove the eggs with a slotted spoon and drain excess water.

5. Divide the sweet potato and kale hash into two plates and top each with poached eggs.

6. Serve hot and enjoy your cholesterol-friendly sweet potato and kale hash with poached eggs!

Nutritional Facts (per serving): Calories: 290 | Total Fat: 11g | Saturated Fat: 2g | Cholesterol: 190mg | Sodium: 160mg | Carbohydrates: 41g | Dietary Fiber: 6g | Sugars: 8g | Protein: 13g

9. Buckwheat Pancakes with Raspberry Sauce

Introduction: These buckwheat pancakes are a gluten-free and fiber-rich option. They're served with a naturally sweet raspberry sauce for a delicious and cholesterol-friendly breakfast.

Prep Time: 10 minutes | Cook Time: 15 minutes | Yield: 2 servings

Ingredients:

For Pancakes:

- 1 cup buckwheat flour
- 2 tablespoons sugar (or sweetener of choice)
- 1 teaspoon baking powder
- 1/2 teaspoon baking soda
- 1/4 teaspoon salt
- 1 cup almond milk (unsweetened)
- 1 large egg
- 1 tablespoon canola oil
- 1 teaspoon vanilla extract

For Raspberry Sauce:

- 1 cup fresh or frozen raspberries
- 2 tablespoons honey
- 1/2 teaspoon lemon zest

Method of Preparation:

For Pancakes:

1. In a mixing bowl, combine buckwheat flour, sugar, baking powder, baking soda, and salt.

2. In another bowl, whisk together almond milk, egg, canola oil, and vanilla extract.

3. Pour the wet ingredients into the dry ingredients and stir until just combined. Do not overmix; it's okay if there are lumps.

4. Heat a non-stick griddle or skillet over medium-high heat. Lightly grease with cooking spray or oil.

5. Pour 1/4 cup portions of pancake batter onto the griddle. Cook until bubbles form on the surface, then flip and cook until golden brown on both sides.

For Raspberry Sauce:

1. In a small saucepan, combine raspberries, honey, and lemon zest.

2. Cook over low heat, stirring occasionally, until the raspberries break down and the sauce thickens, about 5 minutes.

3. Remove from heat and let it cool slightly.

4. Serve the buckwheat pancakes with raspberry sauce drizzled over the top.

5. Enjoy your cholesterol-friendly buckwheat pancakes with raspberry sauce!

Nutritional Facts (per serving, including raspberry sauce): Calories: 350 | Total Fat: 7g | Saturated Fat: 1g | Cholesterol: 55mg | Sodium: 430mg | Carbohydrates: 63g | Dietary Fiber: 9g | Sugars: 21g | Protein: 10g

10. Cottage Cheese and Pineapple Breakfast Bowl

Introduction: This cottage cheese and pineapple breakfast bowl is a high-protein, low-cholesterol option that's both satisfying and refreshing.

Prep Time: 5 minutes | Yield: 1 serving

Ingredients:

- 1 cup low-fat cottage cheese
- 1/2 cup diced fresh pineapple
- 1/4 cup chopped walnuts
- 1 tablespoon honey
- Fresh mint leaves for garnish (optional)

Method of Preparation:

1. In a bowl, spoon low-fat cottage cheese.
2. Top with diced fresh pineapple and chopped walnuts.
3. Drizzle honey over the top for sweetness.
4. Garnish with fresh mint leaves if desired.
5. Serve and enjoy your cholesterol-friendly cottage cheese and pineapple breakfast bowl!

Nutritional Facts (per serving): Calories: 380 | Total Fat: 16g | Saturated Fat: 1.5g | Cholesterol: 10mg | Sodium: 640mg | Carbohydrates: 37g | Dietary Fiber: 3g | Sugars: 27g | Protein: 28g

11. Peanut Butter and Banana Smoothie

Introduction: This creamy and cholesterol-friendly peanut butter and banana smoothie is a quick and nutritious breakfast option that's rich in protein and healthy fats.

Prep Time: 5 minutes | Yield: 2 servings

Ingredients:

- 2 ripe bananas
- 2 tablespoons natural peanut butter
- 1 cup Greek yogurt (low-fat or non-fat)
- 1 cup unsweetened almond milk
- 1 tablespoon honey (optional)
- 1/2 teaspoon vanilla extract
- Ice cubes (optional)

Method of Preparation

1. Peel and slice the ripe bananas.
2. In a blender, combine the banana slices, natural peanut butter, Greek yogurt, unsweetened almond milk, honey (if desired), and vanilla extract.
3. Add ice cubes if you prefer a colder smoothie.
4. Blend until smooth and creamy.
5. Pour into glasses and enjoy your cholesterol-friendly peanut butter and banana smoothie!

Nutritional Facts (per serving): Calories: 280 | Total Fat: 11g | Saturated Fat: 2g | Cholesterol: 5mg | Sodium: 150mg | Carbohydrates: 33g | Dietary Fiber: 4g | Sugars: 19g | Protein: 17g

12. Veggie Omelette with Feta Cheese

Introduction: This vegetable-packed omelette with feta cheese is a protein-rich breakfast option that's low in cholesterol and bursting with flavor.

Prep Time: 10 minutes | Cook Time: 10 minutes | Yield: 2 servings

Ingredients:

- 4 large eggs
- 1/2 cup diced bell peppers (red, green, or yellow)
- 1/4 cup diced onions
- 1/4 cup diced tomatoes
- 1/4 cup crumbled feta cheese (low-fat)
- 2 tablespoons chopped fresh parsley
- Salt and pepper to taste
- Cooking spray

Method of Preparation

- In a bowl, whisk the eggs and season with salt and pepper.
- Heat a non-stick skillet over medium heat and lightly coat it with cooking spray.
- Add diced onions and diced bell peppers to the skillet. Sauté for a few minutes until they soften.
- Pour the whisked eggs into the skillet. Allow them to cook undisturbed for a minute or two.
- Sprinkle diced tomatoes, crumbled feta cheese, and chopped fresh parsley over one half of the omelette.
- Carefully fold the other half of the omelette over the toppings to create a half-moon shape.
- Cook for an additional minute or until the eggs are set and the cheese begins to melt.
- Slide the omelette onto a plate and cut it in half.
- Serve hot and enjoy your cholesterol-friendly veggie omelette with feta cheese!

Nutritional Facts (per serving): Calories: 200 | Total Fat: 12g | Saturated Fat: 5g | Cholesterol: 385mg | Sodium: 290mg | Carbohydrates: 8g | Dietary Fiber: 2g | Sugars: 4g | Protein: 16g

13. Green Smoothie with Kale and Mango

Introduction: This green smoothie with kale and mango is a nutrient-packed breakfast option that's loaded with vitamins and antioxidants while being low in cholesterol.

Prep Time: 5 minutes | Yield: 2 servings

Ingredients:

- 2 cups fresh kale leaves, stems removed
- 1 cup frozen mango chunks
- 1 banana
- 1 cup unsweetened almond milk
- 1/2 cup Greek yogurt (low-fat or non-fat)
- 1 tablespoon honey (optional)
- Ice cubes (optional)

Method of Preparation:

1. Place fresh kale leaves, frozen mango chunks, banana, almond milk, Greek yogurt, and honey (if desired) in a blender.
2. Add ice cubes if you prefer a colder smoothie.
3. Blend until smooth and creamy.
4. Pour into glasses and enjoy your cholesterol-friendly green smoothie with kale and mango!

Nutritional Facts (per serving): Calories: 190 | Total Fat: 3.5g | Saturated Fat: 0g | Cholesterol: 5mg | Sodium: 140mg | Carbohydrates: 36g | Dietary Fiber: 4g | Sugars: 21g | Protein: 6g

14. Vegan Chia Seed Pudding with Berries

Introduction: This vegan chia seed pudding with berries is a creamy and cholesterol-friendly breakfast option that's rich in omega-3 fatty acids and antioxidants.

Prep Time: 5 minutes (plus chilling time) | Yield: 2 servings

Ingredients:

- 1/4 cup chia seeds
- 1 cup unsweetened almond milk
- 1 tablespoon maple syrup (or sweetener of choice)
- 1/2 teaspoon vanilla extract
- 1/2 cup mixed berries (e.g., strawberries, blueberries, raspberries)

Method of Preparation:

In a bowl, whisk together chia seeds, almond milk, maple syrup (or sweetener of choice), and vanilla extract.

Cover the bowl and refrigerate for at least 4 hours or overnight, allowing the chia seeds to absorb the liquid and thicken.

Before serving, stir the chia seed pudding well to break up any clumps.

Spoon the pudding into serving dishes and top with mixed berries.

Enjoy your cholesterol-friendly vegan chia seed pudding with berries!

Nutritional Facts (per serving): Calories: 150 | Total Fat: 7g | Saturated Fat: 0.5g | Cholesterol: 0mg | Sodium: 80mg | Carbohydrates: 21g | Dietary Fiber: 9g | Sugars: 8g | Protein: 4g

15. Broccoli and Tomato Breakfast Wrap

Introduction: This broccoli and tomato breakfast wrap is a savory, cholesterol-friendly option that's perfect for those looking for a healthy and satisfying morning meal.

Prep Time: 10 minutes | Cook Time: 10 minutes | Yield: 2 wraps

Ingredients:

4 large eggs

1 cup broccoli florets, steamed and chopped

1/2 cup diced tomatoes

1/4 cup diced red onions

1/4 cup shredded low-fat cheddar cheese

2 whole-grain tortillas

Salt and pepper to taste

Cooking spray

Method of Preparation

1. In a bowl, whisk the eggs and season with salt and pepper.
2. Heat a non-stick skillet over medium heat and lightly coat it with cooking spray.
3. Add diced red onions and cook for a few minutes until they become translucent.
4. Pour the whisked eggs into the skillet. Cook, stirring gently, until they are just set.
5. Add chopped steamed broccoli, diced tomatoes, and shredded low-fat cheddar cheese to the skillet. Stir until the cheese melts and the vegetables are heated through.
6. Warm the whole-grain tortillas in a dry skillet or microwave for a few seconds.

7. Divide the egg and vegetable mixture evenly between the tortillas.
8. Fold the sides of the tortillas inwards, then roll them up to create wraps.
9. Serve hot and enjoy your cholesterol-friendly broccoli and tomato breakfast wrap!

Nutritional Facts (per wrap): Calories: 280 | Total Fat: 12g | Saturated Fat: 3.5g | Cholesterol: 250mg | Sodium: 370mg | Carbohydrates: 26g | Dietary Fiber: 6g | Sugars: 4g | Protein: 18g

(Note: Nutritional values may vary depending on specific brands and ingredient choices.)

DRINK AND SMOOTHIE

1. Green Tea and Lemon Detox Drink

Introduction: This Green Tea and Lemon Detox Drink is a refreshing way to boost your metabolism and promote a healthy heart. It's packed with antioxidants from green tea and the zesty kick of lemon.

Prep Time: 5 minutes | Yield: 1 serving

Ingredients:

- 1 green tea bag
- 1 cup hot water
- Juice of 1 lemon
- 1 teaspoon honey (optional)

Method of Preparation:

1. Steep the green tea bag in hot water for 3-5 minutes.
2. Remove the tea bag and let the tea cool slightly.
3. Stir in the lemon juice and honey (if desired).
4. Enjoy your cholesterol-friendly Green Tea and Lemon Detox Drink!

Nutritional Facts (per serving, without honey): Calories: 0 | Total Fat: 0g | Saturated Fat: 0g | Cholesterol: 0mg | Sodium: 0mg | Carbohydrates: 0g | Dietary Fiber: 0g | Sugars: 0g | Protein: 0g

2. Berry Blast Smoothie with Flaxseeds

Introduction: This Berry Blast Smoothie is a delicious and cholesterol-friendly way to kickstart your day with a burst of antioxidants and omega-3 fatty acids from flaxseeds.

Prep Time: 5 minutes | Yield: 1 serving |

Ingredients:

- 1 cup mixed berries (e.g., strawberries, blueberries, raspberries)
- 1 ripe banana
- 1 tablespoon ground flaxseeds
- 1 cup unsweetened almond milk
- 1/2 cup Greek yogurt (low-fat or non-fat)
- 1 teaspoon honey (optional)

Method of Preparation:

Place mixed berries, ripe banana, ground flaxseeds, almond milk, Greek yogurt, and honey (if desired) in a blender.

Blend until smooth and creamy.

Pour into a glass and enjoy your cholesterol-friendly Berry Blast Smoothie with Flaxseeds!

Nutritional Facts (per serving, without honey): Calories: 240 | Total Fat: 6g | Saturated Fat: 0.5g | Cholesterol: 5mg | Sodium: 190mg | Carbohydrates: 41g | Dietary Fiber: 9g | Sugars: 23g | Protein: 9g

3. Turmeric and Ginger Immune-Boosting Smoothie

Introduction: This Turmeric and Ginger Immune-Boosting Smoothie is not only delicious but also loaded with anti-inflammatory properties to support your overall health and lower cholesterol.

Prep Time: 5 minutes | Yield: 1 serving

Ingredients:

- 1 ripe banana
- 1/2 cup frozen mango chunks
- 1/2 cup Greek yogurt (low-fat or non-fat)
- 1/2 teaspoon ground turmeric
- 1/2 teaspoon grated fresh ginger
- 1 cup unsweetened almond milk
- 1 teaspoon honey (optional)

Method of Preparation:

1. Place the ripe banana, frozen mango chunks, Greek yogurt, ground turmeric, grated fresh ginger, almond milk, and honey (if desired) in a blender.
2. Blend until smooth and creamy.
3. Pour into a glass and enjoy your cholesterol-friendly Turmeric and Ginger Immune-Boosting Smoothie!

Nutritional Facts (per serving, without honey): Calories: 230 | Total Fat: 2g | Saturated Fat: 0g | Cholesterol: 5mg | Sodium: 210mg | Carbohydrates: 43g | Dietary Fiber: 6g | Sugars: 26g | Protein: 12g

4. Kale and Pineapple Smoothie with Chia Seeds

Introduction: This Kale and Pineapple Smoothie with Chia Seeds is a nutrient-packed powerhouse that's rich in fiber and antioxidants, making it a great choice for reducing cholesterol.

Prep Time: 5 minutes | Yield: 1 serving

Ingredients:

- 1 cup fresh kale leaves, stems removed

- 1 cup diced pineapple (fresh or frozen)
- 1 tablespoon chia seeds
- 1/2 cup coconut water
- 1/2 cup unsweetened coconut milk
- 1 teaspoon honey (optional)

Method of Preparation:

1. Place fresh kale leaves, diced pineapple, chia seeds, coconut water, unsweetened coconut milk, and honey (if desired) in a blender.
2. Blend until smooth and creamy.
3. Pour into a glass and enjoy your cholesterol-friendly Kale and Pineapple Smoothie with Chia Seeds!

Nutritional Facts (per serving, without honey): Calories: 200 | Total Fat: 8g | Saturated Fat: 2g | Cholesterol: 0mg | Sodium: 65mg | Carbohydrates: 34g | Dietary Fiber: 10g Sugars: 16g | Protein: 4g

5. Cucumber and Mint Infused Water

Introduction: This Cucumber and Mint Infused Water is a simple, hydrating drink with a refreshing twist, perfect for keeping your cholesterol in check.

Prep Time: 5 minutes | Yield: 1 serving

Ingredients:

- 1/2 cucumber, thinly sliced
- 5-6 fresh mint leaves
- 1 cup ice-cold water

Method of Preparation:

1. In a glass or pitcher, combine thinly sliced cucumber and fresh mint leaves.
2. Add ice-cold water.
3. Stir gently to infuse the flavors.
4. Serve immediately and enjoy your cholesterol-friendly Cucumber and Mint Infused Water!

Nutritional Facts (per serving): Calories: 0 | Total Fat: 0g | Saturated Fat: 0g | Cholesterol: 0mg | Sodium: 0mg | Carbohydrates: 0g | Dietary Fiber: 0g | Sugars: 0g | Protein: 0g

6. Carrot and Ginger Juice

Introduction: This Carrot and Ginger Juice is a vibrant and cholesterol-friendly drink that's not only refreshing but also packed with vitamins and antioxidants.

Prep Time: 10 minutes | Yield: 1 serving

Ingredients:

- 3 large carrots, peeled and chopped
- 1-inch piece of fresh ginger, peeled
- 1/2 lemon, peeled and seeds removed

Method of Preparation:

1. Run the peeled and chopped carrots, fresh ginger, and peeled lemon through a juicer.
2. Stir the juice to combine the flavors.
3. Serve immediately and enjoy your cholesterol-friendly Carrot and Ginger Juice!

Nutritional Facts (per serving): | Calories: 80 | Total Fat: 0g | Saturated Fat: 0g | Cholesterol: 0mg | Sodium: 100mg | Carbohydrates: 20g | Dietary Fiber: 4g | Sugars: 10g | Protein: 2g

7. Beetroot and Berry Smoothie

Introduction: This Beetroot and Berry Smoothie is a vibrant and cholesterol-friendly option that combines the earthy sweetness of beets with the antioxidant power of berries.

Prep Time: 5 minutes | Yield: 1 serving

Ingredients:

- 1 small cooked beetroot, peeled and diced
- 1/2 cup mixed berries (e.g., strawberries, blueberries, raspberries)
- 1/2 banana
- 1/2 cup unsweetened almond milk
- 1/2 cup Greek yogurt (low-fat or non-fat)
- 1 teaspoon honey (optional)

Method of Preparation:

1. Place the cooked beetroot, mixed berries, banana, almond milk, Greek yogurt, and honey (if desired) in a blender.
2. Blend until smooth and creamy.
3. Pour into a glass and enjoy your cholesterol-friendly Beetroot and Berry Smoothie!

Nutritional Facts (per serving, without honey): Calories: 220 | Total Fat: 2g | Saturated Fat: 0g | Cholesterol: 5mg | Sodium: 210mg | Carbohydrates: 44g | Dietary Fiber: 6g | Sugars: 25g | Protein: 9g

8. Almond Milk and Date Smoothie

Introduction: This Almond Milk and Date Smoothie is a creamy and cholesterol-friendly option that's naturally sweetened with dates and packed with nutrients.

Prep Time: 5 minutes | Yield: 1 serving

Ingredients

- 1 cup unsweetened almond milk
- 4-5 pitted dates
- 1/2 banana
- 1 tablespoon almond butter
- 1/2 teaspoon vanilla extract
- Ice cubes (optional)

Method of Preparation:

1. Place unsweetened almond milk, pitted dates, banana, almond butter, and vanilla extract in a blender.
2. Add ice cubes if you prefer a colder smoothie.
3. Blend until smooth and creamy.
4. Pour into a glass and enjoy your cholesterol-friendly Almond Milk and Date Smoothie!

Nutritional Facts (per serving): Calories: 260 | Total Fat: 9g | Saturated Fat: 0.5g | Cholesterol: 0mg | Sodium: 190mg | Carbohydrates: 47g | Dietary Fiber: 7g | Sugars: 35g | Protein: 4g

9. Papaya and Spinach Green Smoothie

Introduction: This Papaya and Spinach Green Smoothie is a tropical delight packed with vitamins, fiber, and antioxidants, making it a cholesterol-friendly breakfast option.

Prep Time: 5 minutes | Yield: 1 serving

Ingredients:

- 1 cup fresh spinach leaves
- 1/2 cup diced ripe papaya
- 1/2 banana
- 1/2 cup unsweetened coconut water
- 1/2 cup Greek yogurt (low-fat or non-fat)
- 1 teaspoon honey (optional)

Method of Preparation:

1. Place fresh spinach leaves, diced ripe papaya, banana, unsweetened coconut water, Greek yogurt, and honey (if desired) in a blender.
2. Blend until smooth and creamy.
3. Pour into a glass and enjoy your cholesterol-friendly Papaya and Spinach Green Smoothie!

Nutritional Facts (per serving, without honey): Calories: 190 | Total Fat: 1g | Saturated Fat: 0g | Cholesterol: 5mg | Sodium: 190mg | Carbohydrates: 40g | Dietary Fiber: 5g | Sugars: 26g| Protein: 8g

10. Acai Berry Smoothie Bowl with Nuts and Seeds

Introduction: This Acai Berry Smoothie Bowl with Nuts and Seeds is a cholesterol-friendly breakfast that's not only visually appealing but also rich in antioxidants, fiber, and healthy fats.

Prep Time: 10 minutes | Yield: 1 serving

Ingredients

- 1 packet frozen acai puree (unsweetened)
- 1/2 banana
- 1/2 cup mixed berries (e.g., strawberries, blueberries, raspberries)
- 1/4 cup unsweetened almond milk
- Toppings: sliced almonds, chia seeds, hemp seeds, fresh berries, sliced banana

Method of Preparation

1. Blend the frozen acai puree, half a banana, mixed berries, and unsweetened almond milk in a blender until you achieve a thick, smooth consistency.
2. Pour the smoothie into a bowl.
3. Top with sliced almonds, chia seeds, hemp seeds, fresh berries, and sliced banana.
4. Enjoy your cholesterol-friendly Acai Berry Smoothie Bowl with Nuts and Seeds!

Nutritional Facts (per serving): Calories: 380 | Total Fat: 21g | Saturated Fat: 1.5g | Cholesterol: 0mg | Sodium: 50mg | Carbohydrates: 49g | Dietary Fiber: 12g | Sugars: 26g | Protein: 8g

11. Golden Turmeric Latte

Introduction: This Golden Turmeric Latte is a warm, comforting drink infused with anti-inflammatory turmeric and spices, offering a heart-healthy start to your day.

Prep Time: 10 minutes | Cook Time: 5 minutes | Yield: 1 serving

Ingredients:

- 1 cup unsweetened almond milk
- 1/2 teaspoon ground turmeric
- 1/4 teaspoon ground cinnamon
- Pinch of black pepper (enhances turmeric absorption)
- Pinch of ground ginger
- Pinch of ground cardamom
- 1 teaspoon honey (optional)

Method of Preparation:

1. In a small saucepan, heat the unsweetened almond milk over medium heat.
2. Whisk in the ground turmeric, ground cinnamon, black pepper, ground ginger, and ground cardamom.
3. Continue to whisk until the mixture is heated through and well combined. Do not boil.
4. Remove from heat and stir in honey if desired.
5. Pour into a mug and enjoy your cholesterol-friendly Golden Turmeric Latte!

Nutritional Facts (per serving, without honey): Calories: 30 | Total Fat: 1g | Saturated Fat: 0g | Cholesterol: 0mg | Sodium: 170mg | Carbohydrates: 3g | Dietary Fiber: 1g | Sugars: 1g | Protein: 1g

12. Watermelon and Mint Cooler

Introduction: This Watermelon and Mint Cooler is a hydrating and heart-healthy drink that's perfect for hot summer days. It's naturally sweet and refreshing.

Prep Time: 10 minutes | Yield: 2 servings

Ingredients:

- 4 cups fresh watermelon, cubed and deseeded
- Juice of 1 lime
- 8-10 fresh mint leaves
- 1 cup ice cubes

Method of Preparation:

1. Place fresh watermelon cubes, lime juice, fresh mint leaves, and ice cubes in a blender.
2. Blend until smooth and well combined.

3. Pour into glasses and enjoy your cholesterol-friendly Watermelon and Mint Cooler!

Nutritional Facts (per serving): Calories: 50 | Total Fat: 0g | Saturated Fat: 0g | Cholesterol: 0mg | Sodium: 0mg | Carbohydrates: 14g | Dietary Fiber: 1g | Sugars: 10g | Protein: 1g

13. Pomegranate and Blueberry Antioxidant Juice

Introduction: This Pomegranate and Blueberry Antioxidant Juice is a potent blend of two antioxidant-rich fruits that can help lower cholesterol and support heart health.

Prep Time: 10 minutes | Yield: 2 servings

Ingredients:

2 cups fresh pomegranate seeds (or store-bought pomegranate juice)

1 cup fresh blueberries

Juice of 1 lemon

1-2 teaspoons honey (optional)

Method of Preparation:

1. If using fresh pomegranate seeds, place them in a blender and pulse to extract the juice. Strain the juice through a fine mesh strainer into a bowl to remove any seeds.
2. In the same blender, combine the fresh blueberries, lemon juice, and honey (if desired).
3. Blend until smooth.
4. In a pitcher, combine the pomegranate juice and blueberry mixture. Stir well to combine.

5. Serve chilled and enjoy your cholesterol-friendly Pomegranate and Blueberry Antioxidant Juice!

Nutritional Facts (per serving, without honey): Calories: 90 | Total Fat: 0g | Saturated Fat: 0g | Cholesterol: 0mg | Sodium: 0mg | Carbohydrates: 22g | Dietary Fiber: 5g | Sugars: 14g | Protein: 1g

14. Pineapple and Ginger Energizing Drink

Introduction: This Pineapple and Ginger Energizing Drink is a zesty and cholesterol-friendly way to kickstart your morning or recharge your energy levels.

Prep Time: 10 minutes | Yield: 2 servings

Ingredients:

- 2 cups fresh pineapple chunks
- 1-inch piece of fresh ginger, peeled
- Juice of 1 lime
- 1-2 teaspoons honey (optional)
- 1 cup ice cubes

Method of Preparation:

1. Place fresh pineapple chunks, peeled ginger, lime juice, honey (if desired), and ice cubes in a blender.
2. Blend until smooth and well combined.
3. Pour into glasses and enjoy your cholesterol-friendly Pineapple and Ginger Energizing Drink!

Nutritional Facts (per serving, without honey): Calories: 60 | Total Fat: 0g | Saturated Fat: 0g | Cholesterol: 0mg | Sodium: 0mg |

Carbohydrates: 16g | Dietary Fiber: 1g | Sugars: 10g | Protein: 1g

15. Chia Seed Lemonade with a Twist

Introduction: This Chia Seed Lemonade with a Twist is a fun and flavorful way to enjoy a cholesterol-friendly beverage that's rich in omega-3 fatty acids from chia seeds.

Prep Time: 10 minutes (plus chilling time) | Yield: 2 servings

Ingredients:

- 1/4 cup chia seeds
- 1 cup freshly squeezed lemon juice
- 4 cups water
- 1/4 cup honey (or sweetener of choice)
- Sliced lemon and mint leaves for garnish (optional)

Method of Preparation:

1. In a large pitcher, combine chia seeds, freshly squeezed lemon juice, water, and honey (or sweetener of choice).
2. Stir well to mix all the ingredients.
3. Refrigerate the mixture for at least 2 hours, or until the chia seeds have expanded and the mixture thickens.
4. Before serving, stir the chia lemonade well.
5. Pour into glasses, garnish with sliced lemon and mint leaves if desired, and enjoy your cholesterol-friendly Chia Seed Lemonade with a Twist!

Nutritional Facts (per serving, with honey): Calories: 110 | Total Fat: 3.5g | Saturated Fat: 0g | Cholesterol: 0mg | Sodium: 10mg | Carbohydrates: 21g | Dietary Fiber: 5g | Sugars: 15g | Protein: 2g

1. Roasted Chickpeas with Herbs and Spices

Introduction: Roasted Chickpeas with Herbs and Spices are a delicious and crunchy snack that's not only satisfying but also heart-healthy. Chickpeas are packed with fiber and plant-based protein, making them an excellent choice for reducing cholesterol levels.

Prep Time: 10 minutes | Cook Time: 35 minutes | Yield: 4 servings

Ingredients:

- 2 cans (15 ounces each) of chickpeas, drained and rinsed
- 2 tablespoons olive oil
- 1 teaspoon ground cumin
- 1 teaspoon smoked paprika
- 1/2 teaspoon garlic powder
- 1/2 teaspoon onion powder
- Salt and pepper to taste
- Fresh herbs (such as rosemary or thyme) for garnish (optional)

Method of Preparation:

1. Preheat your oven to 400°F (200°C).
2. Pat dry the chickpeas with a paper towel to remove excess moisture.
3. In a bowl, toss the chickpeas with olive oil, cumin, smoked paprika, garlic powder, onion powder, salt, and pepper until well coated.
4. Spread the seasoned chickpeas in a single layer on a baking sheet.
5. Roast in the preheated oven for 30-35 minutes or until they are crispy, shaking the pan occasionally for even cooking.
6. Remove from the oven and let them cool slightly. Garnish with fresh herbs if desired.
7. Serve as a cholesterol-friendly snack.

Nutritional Facts (per serving): Calories: 220 | Total Fat: 7g | Saturated Fat: 1g | Cholesterol: 0mg | Sodium: 290mg | Total Carbohydrates: 31g | Dietary Fiber: 7 | Sugars: 0g | Protein: 8g

2. Sliced Cucumber with Hummus Dip

Introduction: Sliced Cucumber with Hummus Dip is a refreshing and wholesome snack that's perfect for anyone looking to manage their cholesterol levels. Cucumbers are low in calories and provide hydration, while hummus adds a creamy and satisfying element to the dish.

Prep Time: 10 minutes | Cook Time: 0 minutes | Yield: 4 servings

Ingredients:

- 2 large cucumbers, sliced
- 1 cup of hummus (store-bought or homemade)
- Fresh parsley or dill for garnish (optional)

Method of Preparation:

1. Wash and slice the cucumbers into rounds or sticks.
2. Arrange the cucumber slices on a platter.
3. Serve with a bowl of hummus for dipping.
4. Garnish with fresh herbs if desired.
5. Enjoy this light and cholesterol-friendly snack!

Nutritional Facts (per serving, including hummus): Calories: 130 | Total Fat: 6g | Saturated Fat: 1g | Cholesterol: 0mg | Sodium: 260mg | Total Carbohydrates: 15g | Dietary Fiber: 5g | Sugars: 2g | Protein: 6g

3. Air-Popped Popcorn with Nutritional Yeast

Introduction: Air-Popped Popcorn with Nutritional Yeast is a guilt-free and tasty way to enjoy a classic snack while promoting heart health. Nutritional yeast adds a cheesy flavor without the saturated fat found in traditional cheese.

Prep Time: 5 minutes | Cook Time: 5 minutes | Yield: 4 servings

Ingredients:

- 1/2 cup popcorn kernels
- 2 tablespoons nutritional yeast
- 1 tablespoon olive oil (optional)
- Salt to taste

Method of Preparation

1. Pop the popcorn using an air popper. If using a stovetop method, use minimal oil.
2. While the popcorn is hot, sprinkle it with nutritional yeast, salt, and olive oil if desired.
3. Toss well to coat evenly.
4. Serve immediately as a cholesterol-friendly snack.

Nutritional Facts (per serving, with olive oil): Calories: 80 | Total Fat: 3g | Saturated Fat: 0.5g Cholesterol: 0mg | Sodium: 150mg | Total Carbohydrates: 12g | Dietary Fiber: 3g | Sugars: 0g | Protein: 2g

4. Mixed Nuts and Dried Cranberries

Introduction: Mixed Nuts and Dried Cranberries is a heart-healthy snack that combines the richness of nuts with the tangy sweetness of cranberries. Nuts are high in monounsaturated fats, which can help lower bad cholesterol levels.

Prep Time: 5 minutes | Cook Time: 0 minutes | Yield: 4 servings

Ingredients:

- 1 cup mixed nuts (e.g., almonds, walnuts, pistachios)
- 1/2 cup dried cranberries

Method of Preparation:

- Simply combine the mixed nuts and dried cranberries in a bowl.
- Toss them together until well mixed.
- Portion into individual servings.
- Enjoy this nutritious and cholesterol-friendly snack.

Nutritional Facts (per serving): Calories: 200| Total Fat: 14g | Saturated Fat: 1.5g | Cholesterol: 0mg | Sodium: 5mg | Total Carbohydrates: 16g | Dietary Fiber: 3g | Sugars: 10g | Protein: 5g

5. Carrot Sticks with Guacamole

Introduction: Carrot Sticks with Guacamole is a delightful way to enjoy the creamy goodness of avocados while getting a dose of vitamins and fiber from carrots. Avocados are rich in heart-healthy monounsaturated fats.

Prep Time: 10 minutes | Cook Time: 0 minutes | Yield: 4 servings

Ingredients:

- 4 large carrots, peeled and cut into sticks
- 2 ripe avocados
- 1 lime, juiced
- 1/4 cup diced red onion
- 1/4 cup diced tomato
- 1 clove garlic, minced
- Salt and pepper to taste
- Fresh cilantro for garnish (optional)

Method of Preparation:

1. In a bowl, mash the avocados and mix them with lime juice, red onion, tomato, and garlic.
2. Season with salt and pepper to taste.
3. Arrange the carrot sticks on a platter.
4. Serve the carrot sticks with guacamole.
5. Garnish with fresh cilantro if desired.
6. Enjoy this nutritious, cholesterol-friendly snack.

Nutritional Facts (per serving, including guacamole): Calories: 190 | Total Fat: 14g | Saturated Fat: 2g | Cholesterol: 0mg | Sodium: 80mg | Total Carbohydrates: 17g | Dietary Fiber: 9g | Sugars: 4g | Protein: 3g

6. Edamame with Sea Salt

Introduction: Edamame with Sea Salt is a simple and nutritious snack that's rich in plant-based protein and low in cholesterol. Edamame, young soybeans, are a heart-healthy choice that can help lower bad cholesterol levels.

Prep Time: 5 minutes | Cook Time: 5 minutes | Yield: 4 servings

Ingredients

- 2 cups edamame (frozen or fresh)
- Sea salt to taste

Method of Preparation

1. If using frozen edamame, steam or boil them according to package instructions until tender.
2. Drain and pat them dry with a paper towel.
3. Sprinkle sea salt over the edamame while they are still warm.
4. Toss to coat evenly.
5. Serve as a cholesterol-friendly snack.

Nutritional Facts (per serving): Calories: 100 | Total Fat: 3.5g | Saturated Fat: 0.5g | Cholesterol: 0mg | Sodium: 5mg | Total Carbohydrates: 8g | Dietary Fiber: 4g | Sugars: 2g | Protein: 8g

7. Brown Rice Cakes with Almond Butter

Introduction: Brown Rice Cakes with Almond Butter offer a satisfying and wholesome option for snacking while helping to manage cholesterol levels. Almond butter is rich in monounsaturated fats and can contribute to a heart-healthy diet.

Prep Time: 5 minutes | Cook Time: 0 minutes | Yield: 4 servings

Ingredients:

- 4 brown rice cakes
- 1/2 cup almond butter
- Fresh berries for topping (optional)

Method of Preparation:

1. Spread almond butter evenly on each brown rice cake.
2. Top with fresh berries if desired.
3. Serve as a cholesterol-friendly snack.

Nutritional Facts (per serving): Calories: 220 | Total Fat: 15g | Saturated Fat: 1.5g | Cholesterol: 0mg | Sodium: 0mg | Total Carbohydrates: 15g | Dietary Fiber: 3g | Sugars: 2g | Protein: 6g

8. Greek Yogurt with Honey and Walnuts

Introduction: Greek Yogurt with Honey and Walnuts is a creamy and satisfying snack that's rich in protein and healthy fats. Greek yogurt provides probiotics that can support heart health, and walnuts offer omega-3 fatty acids.

Prep Time: 5 minutes | Cook Time: 0 minutes | Yield: 4 servings

Ingredients

- 2 cups Greek yogurt (low-fat or full-fat)
- 4 tablespoons honey
- 1/2 cup chopped walnuts

Method of Preparation

1. Divide Greek yogurt into four serving bowls.
2. Drizzle each serving with 1 tablespoon of honey.
3. Sprinkle with chopped walnuts.
4. Serve as a cholesterol-friendly snack.|

Nutritional Facts (per serving): Calories: 260 | Total Fat: 14g | Saturated Fat: 2g | Cholesterol: 10mg | Sodium: 40mg | Total Carbohydrates:

23g | Dietary Fiber: 1g | Sugars: 20g | Protein: 15g

9. Sliced Apple with Peanut Butter

Introduction: Sliced Apple with Peanut Butter is a classic and nutritious combination that's perfect for a heart-healthy snack. Apples provide fiber, while peanut butter offers healthy fats and protein.

Prep Time: 5 minutes | Cook Time: 0 minutes | Yield: 4 servings

Ingredients

- 2 large apples, sliced
- 1/2 cup natural peanut butter (unsweetened)

Method of Preparation

1. Slice the apples into thin rounds or wedges.
2. Serve with a side of natural peanut butter for dipping.
3. Enjoy this balanced and cholesterol-friendly snack.

Nutritional Facts (per serving): Calories: 250 | Total Fat: 17g | Saturated Fat: 3g | Cholesterol: 0mg | Sodium: 130mg | Total Carbohydrates: 20g | Dietary Fiber: 5g | Sugars: 11g | Protein: 7g

10. Baked Sweet Potato Fries with Paprika

Introduction: Baked Sweet Potato Fries with Paprika are a flavorful and cholesterol-friendly alternative to traditional fries. Sweet potatoes are rich in fiber and antioxidants, making them a heart-healthy choice.

Prep Time: 10 minutes | Cook Time: 25 minutes | Yield: 4 servings

Ingredients

- 2 large sweet potatoes, cut into fries
- 2 tablespoons olive oil
- 1 teaspoon paprika
- Salt and pepper to taste

Method of Preparation

1. Preheat your oven to 425°F (220°C).
2. In a large bowl, toss the sweet potato fries with olive oil, paprika, salt, and pepper until well coated.
3. Arrange the fries in a single layer on a baking sheet.
4. Bake for 20-25 minutes, flipping the fries halfway through, or until they are golden and crispy.
5. Serve as a delicious, cholesterol-friendly snack.

Nutritional Facts (per serving): Calories: 160 | Total Fat: 7g | Saturated Fat: 1g | Cholesterol: 0mg | Sodium: 70mg | Total Carbohydrates: 24g | Dietary Fiber: 4g | Sugars: 5g | Protein: 2g

11. Veggie Sticks with Tzatziki Sauce

Introduction: Veggie Sticks with Tzatziki Sauce are a light and refreshing way to enjoy crunchy vegetables while benefiting from the probiotics in Greek yogurt. Tzatziki sauce is a creamy and heart-healthy dip.

Prep Time: 15 minutes | Cook Time: 0 minutes | Yield: 4 servings

Ingredients

- 2 cups Greek yogurt (low-fat or full-fat)
- 1 cucumber, grated and drained
- 2 cloves garlic, minced
- 1 tablespoon fresh dill, chopped
- 1 tablespoon lemon juice
- Salt and pepper to taste
- Assorted vegetable sticks (carrots, cucumbers, bell peppers, celery, etc.)

Method of Preparation

1. In a bowl, combine Greek yogurt, grated cucumber, minced garlic, fresh dill, lemon juice, salt, and pepper.
2. Mix well to make the tzatziki sauce.
3. Prepare the assorted vegetable sticks for dipping.
4. Serve the vegetable sticks with tzatziki sauce.
5. Enjoy this wholesome and cholesterol-friendly snack.

Nutritional Facts (per serving, including tzatziki sauce): Calories: 130 | Total Fat: 3.5g | Saturated Fat: 2g | Cholesterol: 10mg | Sodium: 70mg | Total Carbohydrates: 12g | Dietary Fiber: 2g | Sugars: 6g | Protein: 12g

12. Quinoa and Black Bean Salad Cups

Introduction: Quinoa and Black Bean Salad Cups are a nutritious and cholesterol-friendly snack that combines the protein and fiber of black beans with the wholesome goodness of quinoa.

Prep Time: 15 minutes | Cook Time: 15 minutes | Yield: 4 servings

Ingredients:

- 1 cup quinoa, rinsed
- 2 cups water or vegetable broth
- 1 can (15 ounces) black beans, drained and rinsed
- 1 cup diced tomatoes
- 1/2 cup diced red bell pepper
- 1/2 cup diced cucumber
- 1/4 cup chopped fresh cilantro
- 2 tablespoons olive oil
- 2 tablespoons lime juice
- Salt and pepper to taste
- Lettuce leaves for serving (optional)

Method of Preparation:

1. In a saucepan, combine quinoa and water (or vegetable broth). Bring to a boil, then reduce heat, cover, and simmer for 12-15 minutes until quinoa is cooked and liquid is absorbed. Fluff with a fork and let it cool.
2. In a large bowl, combine cooked quinoa, black beans, diced tomatoes, red bell pepper, cucumber, and fresh cilantro.
3. In a small bowl, whisk together olive oil, lime juice, salt, and pepper. Pour this dressing over the quinoa mixture and toss to combine.
4. If desired, serve the quinoa and black bean salad in lettuce cups.
5. Enjoy this nutritious and cholesterol-friendly snack.

Nutritional Facts (per serving): Calories: 330 | Total Fat: 10g | Saturated Fat: 1.5g | Cholesterol: 0mg | Sodium: 240mg | Total Carbohydrates: 50g | Dietary Fiber: 10g | Sugars: 2g | Protein: 11g

13. Trail Mix with Dark Chocolate and Almonds

Introduction: Trail Mix with Dark Chocolate and Almonds is a delicious and satisfying snack that combines heart-healthy almonds with the antioxidant benefits of dark chocolate.

Prep Time: 5 minutes | Cook Time: 0 minutes | Yield: 4 servings

Ingredients:

- 1 cup raw almonds
- 1/2 cup dark chocolate chips or chunks (70% cocoa or higher)
- 1/2 cup dried cranberries
- 1/4 cup unsalted pumpkin seeds (pepitas)
- 1/4 cup unsalted sunflower seeds

Method of Preparation:

1. In a bowl, combine almonds, dark chocolate chips, dried cranberries, pumpkin seeds, and sunflower seeds.
2. Toss to mix all ingredients evenly.
3. Portion into individual servings.
4. Enjoy this delicious and cholesterol-friendly snack.

Nutritional Facts (per serving): Calories: 320 | Total Fat: 20g | Saturated Fat: 4g | Cholesterol: 0mg | Sodium: 10mg | Total Carbohydrates: 33g | Dietary Fiber: 6g | Sugars: 20g || Protein: 7g

14. Seaweed Snacks with Sesame

Introduction: Seaweed Snacks with Sesame provide a unique and nutritious option for snacking. Seaweed is naturally low in cholesterol and calories, while sesame seeds add a delightful crunch and flavor.

Prep Time: 5 minutes | Time: 5 minutes | Yield: 4 servings

Ingredients:

- 4 sheets of roasted seaweed snacks
- 1 tablespoon sesame seeds
- 1/2 teaspoon low-sodium soy sauce (optional)

Method of Preparation:

1. If desired, lightly brush each seaweed sheet with low-sodium soy sauce for added flavor (this is optional).
2. Sprinkle sesame seeds evenly over the seaweed sheets.
3. Gently press the sesame seeds onto the seaweed.
4. Cut or tear the seaweed sheets into bite-sized pieces.
5. Enjoy this unique and cholesterol-friendly snack.

Nutritional Facts (per serving): Calories: 35 | Total Fat: 2g | Saturated Fat: 0g | Cholesterol: 0mg | Sodium: 60mg | Total Carbohydrates: 3g | Dietary Fiber: 1g | Sugars: 0g | Protein: 2g

15. Spicy Roasted Cauliflower Bites

Introduction: Spicy Roasted Cauliflower Bites are a flavorful and low-cholesterol snack that's perfect for those who enjoy a bit of heat. Cauliflower is rich in fiber and can be a heart-healthy alternative to traditional snacks.

Prep Time: 10 minutes | Cook Time: 25 minutes | Yield: 4 servings

Ingredients:

- 1 head of cauliflower, cut into florets
- 2 tablespoons olive oil
- 1 teaspoon smoked paprika
- 1/2 teaspoon cayenne pepper (adjust to taste)
- Salt and pepper to taste
- Fresh cilantro or parsley for garnish (optional)

Method of Preparation:

1. Preheat your oven to 425°F (220°C).
2. In a bowl, toss cauliflower florets with olive oil, smoked paprika, cayenne pepper, salt, and pepper until well coated.
3. Spread the seasoned cauliflower in a single layer on a baking sheet.
4. Roast in the preheated oven for 25-30 minutes or until the cauliflower is tender and slightly crispy, tossing halfway through.
5. Remove from the oven and garnish with fresh cilantro or parsley if desired.
6. Enjoy these spicy roasted cauliflower bites as a cholesterol-friendly snack.

Nutritional Facts (per serving): Calories: 80 | Total Fat: 5g | Saturated Fat: 0.5g | Cholesterol: 0mg | Sodium: 25mg | Total Carbohydrates: 8g | Dietary Fiber: 3g | Sugars: 3g | Protein: 2g

1. Lentil and Vegetable Curry

Introduction: Lentil and Vegetable Curry is a hearty and cholesterol-friendly dish packed with plant-based protein and fiber. This flavorful curry is a perfect choice for a heart-healthy meal.

Prep Time: 15 minutes | Cook Time: 30 minutes | Yield: 4 servings

Ingredients:

- 1 cup dried brown lentils
- 2 cups water
- 2 tablespoons olive oil
- 1 onion, chopped
- 2 cloves garlic, minced
- 1 tablespoon ginger, minced
- 2 carrots, diced
- 2 potatoes, diced
- 1 bell pepper, diced
- 1 can (14 ounces) diced tomatoes
- 2 tablespoons curry powder
- 1 teaspoon cumin
- 1/2 teaspoon turmeric
- Salt and pepper to taste
- Fresh cilantro for garnish (optional)

Method of Preparation

1. Rinse lentils and cook them in 2 cups of water until tender, about 20-25 minutes. Drain and set aside.
2. In a large pot, heat olive oil over medium heat. Add onions, garlic, and ginger. Sauté until fragrant.
3. Add carrots, potatoes, and bell pepper. Cook for 5 minutes.
4. Stir in the diced tomatoes, curry powder, cumin, turmeric, salt, and pepper. Cook for another 5 minutes.
5. Add the cooked lentils to the pot and simmer for 10 minutes.

6. Garnish with fresh cilantro if desired.
7. Serve this delicious lentil and vegetable curry as a cholesterol-friendly meal.

Nutritional Facts (per serving): Calories: 350 | Total Fat: 7g | Saturated Fat: 1g | Cholesterol: 0mg | Sodium: 600mg | Total Carbohydrates: 59g | Dietary Fiber: 17g | Sugars: 8g | Protein: 15g

2. Chickpea and Spinach Pasta

Introduction: Chickpea and Spinach Pasta is a delicious and heart-healthy dish that combines the goodness of chickpeas and spinach with whole wheat pasta. It's a satisfying option for those looking to manage cholesterol levels.

Prep Time: 10 minutes | Cook Time: 15 minutes | Yield: 4 servings

Ingredients:

- 8 ounces whole wheat pasta
- 1 can (15 ounces) chickpeas, drained and rinsed
- 2 tablespoons olive oil
- 3 cloves garlic, minced
- 6 cups fresh spinach
- 1/2 teaspoon red pepper flakes (adjust to taste)
- Salt and pepper to taste
- Grated Parmesan cheese for garnish (optional)

Method of Preparation:

1. Cook the whole wheat pasta according to package instructions. Drain and set aside.

2. In a large skillet, heat olive oil over medium heat. Add minced garlic and red pepper flakes. Sauté for 1 minute.
3. Add chickpeas and sauté for another 2 minutes.
4. Stir in fresh spinach and cook until wilted.
5. Toss in the cooked pasta and combine well.
6. Season with salt and pepper to taste.
7. Serve hot, garnished with grated Parmesan cheese if desired.

Nutritional Facts (per serving): Calories: 350 | Total Fat: 10g | Saturated Fat: 1.5g | Cholesterol: 0mg | Sodium: 330mg | Total Carbohydrates: 55g | Dietary Fiber: 11g | Sugars: 3g | Protein: 15g

3. Quinoa and Black Bean Stuffed Bell Peppers

Introduction: Quinoa and Black Bean Stuffed Bell Peppers are a nutritious and satisfying meal that combines the protein and fiber of black beans with the wholesome goodness of quinoa, all packed inside colorful bell peppers.

Prep Time: 20 minutes | Cook Time: 40 minutes | Yield: 4 servings (2 stuffed peppers each)

Ingredients

- 4 large bell peppers, any color
- 1 cup quinoa, rinsed
- 2 cups vegetable broth
- 1 can (15 ounces) black beans, drained and rinsed
- 1 cup corn kernels (fresh or frozen)
- 1 cup diced tomatoes
- 1 teaspoon chili powder
- 1/2 teaspoon cumin
- Salt and pepper to taste

- Shredded cheddar cheese for topping (optional)

Method of Preparation:

1. Preheat your oven to 375°F (190°C).
2. Cut the tops off the bell peppers and remove the seeds and membranes. Set them aside.
3. In a saucepan, combine quinoa and vegetable broth. Bring to a boil, then reduce heat, cover, and simmer for 15-20 minutes until quinoa is cooked and liquid is absorbed. Fluff with a fork and let it cool.
4. In a mixing bowl, combine cooked quinoa, black beans, corn, diced tomatoes, chili powder, cumin, salt, and pepper.
5. Stuff each bell pepper with the quinoa and black bean mixture.
6. Place the stuffed peppers in a baking dish, and optionally, top each with shredded cheddar cheese.
7. Bake for 20-25 minutes or until the peppers are tender.
8. Serve as a nutritious and cholesterol-friendly meal.

Nutritional Facts (per serving, 2 stuffed peppers each): Calories: 380 | Total Fat: 3g | Saturated Fat: 0.5g | Cholesterol: 0mg | Sodium: 490mg | Total Carbohydrates: 75g | Dietary Fiber: 15g | | Sugars: 9g | Protein: 15g

4. Whole Wheat Spaghetti with Garlic and Broccoli

Introduction: Whole Wheat Spaghetti with Garlic and Broccoli is a simple and wholesome pasta dish that's rich in fiber and flavor. Whole wheat pasta and broccoli make this a cholesterol-friendly choice.

Prep Time: 10 minutes | Cook Time: 15 minutes | Yield: 4 servings

Ingredients:

- 8 ounces whole wheat spaghetti
- 2 cups broccoli florets
- 3 tablespoons olive oil
- 3 cloves garlic, minced
- Red pepper flakes to taste (optional)
- Salt and pepper to taste
- Grated Parmesan cheese for garnish (optional)

Method of Preparation:

1. Cook the whole wheat spaghetti according to package instructions. During the last 3 minutes of cooking, add the broccoli florets to the boiling water with the pasta.
2. Drain the pasta and broccoli, reserving a small amount of pasta water.
3. In a large skillet, heat olive oil over medium heat. Add minced garlic and red pepper flakes (if using). Sauté for 1-2 minutes.
4. Add the cooked pasta and broccoli to the skillet and toss to combine. If needed, add a bit of reserved pasta water to create a light sauce.
5. Season with salt and pepper to taste.
6. Serve hot, garnished with grated Parmesan cheese if desired.

Nutritional Facts (per serving): Calories: 300 | Total Fat: 11g | Saturated Fat: 1.5g | Cholesterol: 0mg | Sodium: 40mg | Total Carbohydrates: 45g | Dietary Fiber: 7g | Sugars: 2g | Protein: 9g

5. Brown Rice and Mixed Vegetable Stir-Fry

Introduction: Brown Rice and Mixed Vegetable Stir-Fry is a wholesome and cholesterol-friendly meal that combines the nuttiness of brown rice with a variety of colorful vegetables, all stir-fried in a savory sauce.

Prep Time: 15 minutes | Cook Time: 20 minutes | Yield: 4 servings

Ingredients

- 2 cups cooked brown rice
- 2 tablespoons vegetable oil
- 1 onion, sliced
- 2 cloves garlic, minced
- 2 cups mixed vegetables (e.g., bell peppers, broccoli, snap peas, carrots)
- 1/4 cup low-sodium soy sauce
- 1 tablespoon rice vinegar
- 1 tablespoon honey or maple syrup
- 1/2 teaspoon ginger, minced
- Sesame seeds for garnish (optional)

Method of Preparation

1. In a wok or large skillet, heat vegetable oil over medium-high heat.
2. Add sliced onion and minced garlic. Sauté for 2-3 minutes until fragrant.
3. Add the mixed vegetables and stir-fry for 5-7 minutes until they are tender-crisp.
4. In a small bowl, whisk together low-sodium soy sauce, rice vinegar, honey or maple syrup, and minced ginger.
5. Add the cooked brown rice to the wok or skillet, and pour the sauce over the rice and vegetables.
6. Stir-fry for an additional 3-4 minutes until everything is well-coated and heated through.
7. Serve hot, garnished with sesame seeds if desired.

Nutritional Facts (per serving): Calories: 320 | Total Fat: 7g | Saturated Fat: 0.5g | Cholesterol: 0mg | Sodium: 530mg | Total Carbohydrates: 58g | Dietary Fiber: 7g | Sugars: 8g | Protein: 7g

6. Black Bean and Corn Salsa Salad

Introduction: Black Bean and Corn Salsa Salad is a refreshing and nutritious dish that combines the protein of black beans with the sweetness of corn and a zesty salsa dressing. It's a delightful choice for a heart-healthy salad.

Prep Time: 15 minutes | Cook Time: 0 minutes | Yield: 4 servings

Ingredients:

- 2 cans (15 ounces each) black beans, drained and rinsed
- 2 cups frozen corn kernels, thawed
- 1 red bell pepper, diced
- 1/2 red onion, finely chopped
- 1 jalapeño pepper, seeded and minced (optional, for heat)
- 1/4 cup fresh cilantro, chopped
- 1/4 cup lime juice
- 2 tablespoons olive oil
- 1 teaspoon cumin
- Salt and pepper to taste
- Avocado slices for garnish (optional)

Method of Preparation:

1. In a large mixing bowl, combine black beans, thawed corn, diced red bell pepper,

chopped red onion, minced jalapeño (if using), and chopped cilantro.
2. In a separate small bowl, whisk together lime juice, olive oil, cumin, salt, and pepper to make the dressing.
3. Pour the dressing over the bean and corn mixture, and toss to combine.
4. Let the salad sit for about 10 minutes to allow flavors to meld.
5. Serve chilled, garnished with avocado slices if desired.

Nutritional Facts (per serving): Calories: 290 | Total Fat: 7g | Saturated Fat: 1g | Cholesterol: 0mg | Sodium: 390mg | Total Carbohydrates: 50g | Dietary Fiber: 14g | Sugars: 5g | Protein: 13g

7. Red Lentil Soup with Turmeric and Cumin

Introduction: Red Lentil Soup with Turmeric and Cumin is a warm and comforting dish that's not only delicious but also rich in plant-based protein and fiber. Turmeric and cumin add flavor and potential anti-inflammatory benefits.

Prep Time: 10 minutes | Cook Time: 25 minutes | Yield: 4 servings

Ingredients:

- 1 cup red lentils, rinsed
- 1 onion, chopped
- 2 cloves garlic, minced
- 1 carrot, diced
- 1 teaspoon ground turmeric
- 1 teaspoon ground cumin
- 6 cups vegetable broth
- Salt and pepper to taste

- Fresh cilantro for garnish (optional)

Method of Preparation:

1. In a large pot, heat a bit of vegetable broth or water over medium heat. Add chopped onion and sauté for 3-4 minutes until softened.
2. Add minced garlic, diced carrot, ground turmeric, and ground cumin. Sauté for another 2 minutes.
3. Add red lentils and vegetable broth. Bring to a boil, then reduce heat, cover, and simmer for 15-20 minutes until lentils are tender.
4. Use an immersion blender or regular blender to puree the soup until smooth.
5. Season with salt and pepper to taste.
6. Serve hot, garnished with fresh cilantro if desired.

Nutritional Facts (per serving): Calories: 220 | Total Fat: 1g | Saturated Fat: 0g | Cholesterol: 0mg | Sodium: 950mg | Total Carbohydrates: 40g | Dietary Fiber: 8g | Sugars: 5g | Protein: 14g

8. Spinach and Cannellini Bean Spaghetti

Introduction: Spinach and Cannellini Bean Spaghetti is a light and nutritious pasta dish that combines the creaminess of cannellini beans with the goodness of spinach. It's a heart-healthy option that's quick to prepare.

Prep Time: 10 minutes | Cook Time: 15 minutes | Yield: 4 servings

Ingredients:

- 8 ounces whole wheat spaghetti
- 2 tablespoons olive oil
- 2 cloves garlic, minced

- 1 can (15 ounces) cannellini beans, drained and rinsed
- 4 cups fresh spinach
- Juice of 1 lemon
- Salt and pepper to taste
- Grated Parmesan cheese for garnish (optional)

Method of Preparation:

1. Cook the whole wheat spaghetti according to package instructions. Drain and set aside.
2. In a large skillet, heat olive oil over medium heat. Add minced garlic and sauté for 1-2 minutes until fragrant.
3. Add cannellini beans and cook for 3-4 minutes until heated through.
4. Stir in fresh spinach and cook until wilted.
5. Toss in the cooked spaghetti and lemon juice. Mix well.
6. Season with salt and pepper to taste.
7. Serve hot, garnished with grated Parmesan cheese if desired.

Nutritional Facts (per serving): Calories: 330 | Total Fat: 7g | Saturated Fat: 1g |Cholesterol: 0mg | Sodium: 60mg | Total Carbohydrates: 55g | Dietary Fiber: 9g | Sugars: 2g | Protein: 15g

Prep Time: 15 minutes | Cook Time: 30 minutes | Yield: 4 servings

Ingredients:

- 1 teaspoon paprika
- Salt and pepper to taste
- Chopped fresh cilantro for garnish (optional)

Method of Preparation:

1. In a large pot, heat a bit of vegetable broth or water over medium heat. Add chopped onion and sauté for 3-4 minutes until softened.
2. Add minced garlic and diced red bell pepper. Sauté for another 2 minutes.
3. Add black beans, kidney beans, pinto beans, diced tomatoes, chili powder, cumin, paprika, salt, and pepper. Stir well.
4. Simmer the chili for 20-25 minutes, allowing flavors to meld and the chili to thicken.
5. Serve hot, garnished with chopped fresh cilantro if desired.

Nutritional Facts (per serving): Calories: 320 | Total Fat: 2g | Saturated Fat: 0g | Cholesterol: 0mg | Sodium: 790mg | Total Carbohydrates: 62g | Dietary Fiber: 20g | Sugars: 8g | Protein: 18g

9. Three-Bean Chili with Tomatoes

Introduction: Three-Bean Chili with Tomatoes is a hearty and flavorful dish that's loaded with protein and fiber from a trio of beans. This cholesterol-friendly chili is perfect for a satisfying meal.

10. Barley and Mushroom Risotto

Introduction: Barley and Mushroom Risotto is a comforting and heart-healthy dish that swaps traditional Arborio rice with fiber-rich barley. It's a creamy and flavorful meal.

Prep Time: 10 minutes | Cook Time: 45 minutes | Yield: 4 servings

Ingredients

- 1 cup pearl barley
- 3 cups vegetable broth
- 2 tablespoons olive oil
- 1 onion, chopped
- 2 cloves garlic, minced
- 8 ounces mushrooms, sliced
- 1/2 cup dry white wine (optional)
- 1/4 cup grated Parmesan cheese (optional)
- Salt and pepper to taste
- Fresh parsley for garnish (optional)

Method of Preparation:

1. In a saucepan, bring the vegetable broth to a simmer and keep it warm.
2. In a separate large skillet, heat olive oil over medium heat. Add chopped onion and sauté for 3-4 minutes until softened.
3. Add minced garlic and sliced mushrooms. Sauté for another 5 minutes until mushrooms are browned.
4. Add pearl barley to the skillet and stir for 1-2 minutes until it's well-coated with oil and slightly toasted.
5. If using, pour in the dry white wine and stir until it's mostly absorbed.
6. Begin adding the warm vegetable broth to the skillet, one ladle at a time, stirring frequently. Allow each ladle of broth to be absorbed before adding the next.
7. Continue this process until the barley is tender and creamy, which should take about 35-40 minutes.
8. If desired, stir in grated Parmesan cheese.
9. Season with salt and pepper to taste.
10. Serve hot, garnished with fresh parsley if desired.

Nutritional Facts (per serving without Parmesan cheese): Calories: 230 | Total Fat: 6g | Saturated Fat: 1g | Cholesterol: 0mg | Sodium: 400mg | Total Carbohydrates: 37g | Dietary Fiber: 7g | Sugars: 3g | Protein: 6g

11. Quinoa and Black-Eyed Pea Salad

Introduction: Quinoa and Black Eyed Pea Salad is a nutritious and protein-packed dish that combines the nutty flavor of quinoa with the earthy goodness of black-eyed peas. It's a perfect choice for a light and cholesterol-friendly meal.

Prep Time: 15 minutes | Cook Time: 20 minutes | Yield: 4 servings

Ingredients

- 1 cup quinoa, rinsed
- 2 cups vegetable broth
- 1 can (15 ounces) black-eyed peas, drained and rinsed
- 1 red bell pepper, diced
- 1/2 red onion, finely chopped
- 1/4 cup fresh parsley, chopped
- Juice of 1 lemon
- 2 tablespoons olive oil
- Salt and pepper to taste

Method of Preparation

1. In a saucepan, combine quinoa and vegetable broth. Bring to a boil, then reduce heat, cover, and simmer for 15-20 minutes until quinoa is cooked and liquid is absorbed. Fluff with a fork and let it cool.
2. In a large mixing bowl, combine cooked quinoa, black-eyed peas, diced red bell pepper, chopped red onion, and fresh parsley.
3. In a small bowl, whisk together the lemon juice, olive oil, salt, and pepper.

4. Pour the dressing over the quinoa and bean mixture and toss to combine.
5. Serve chilled as a refreshing and cholesterol-friendly salad.

Nutritional Facts (per serving): Calories: 290 | Total Fat: 8g | Saturated Fat: 1g | Cholesterol: 0mg | Sodium: 580mg | Total Carbohydrates: 45g | Dietary Fiber: 8g | Sugars: 3g | Protein: 10g

12. Whole Grain Penne with Tomato and Basil

Introduction: Whole Grain Penne with Tomato and Basil is a simple and flavorful pasta dish that features the goodness of whole grains, fresh tomatoes, and aromatic basil. It's a cholesterol-friendly meal that's easy to prepare.

Prep Time: 10 minutes | Cook Time: 15 minutes | Yield: 4 servings

Ingredients:

- 8 ounces whole grain penne pasta
- 2 tablespoons olive oil
- 2 cloves garlic, minced
- 4 cups fresh tomatoes, diced
- 1/2 cup fresh basil leaves, chopped
- Salt and pepper to taste
- Grated Parmesan cheese for garnish (optional)

Method of Preparation:

1. Cook the whole grain penne pasta according to package instructions. Drain and set aside.

2. In a large skillet, heat olive oil over medium heat. Add minced garlic and sauté for 1-2 minutes until fragrant.
3. Add diced fresh tomatoes and chopped basil. Cook for 5-7 minutes until the tomatoes are softened.
4. Toss in the cooked penne pasta and mix well.
5. Season with salt and pepper to taste.
6. Serve hot, garnished with grated Parmesan cheese if desired.

Nutritional Facts (per serving): Calories: 290 | Total Fat: 8g | Saturated Fat: 1g | Cholesterol: 0mg | Sodium: 10mg | Total Carbohydrates: 48g | Dietary Fiber: 7g | Sugars: 5g | Protein: 10g

13. Sweet Potato and Black Bean Tacos

Introduction: Sweet Potato and Black Bean Tacos are a flavorful and cholesterol-friendly twist on traditional tacos. These tacos combine the sweetness of roasted sweet potatoes with the protein of black beans.

Prep Time: 15 minutes | Cook Time: 25 minutes | Yield: 4 servings

Ingredients

- 2 large sweet potatoes, peeled and diced
- 2 tablespoons olive oil
- 1 teaspoon chili powder
- 1/2 teaspoon cumin
- Salt and pepper to taste
- 1 can (15 ounces) black beans, drained and rinsed
- 8 small whole wheat tortillas
- Salsa, avocado slices, and fresh cilantro for garnish (optional)

Method of Preparation

1. Preheat your oven to 425°F (220°C).
2. In a bowl, toss diced sweet potatoes with olive oil, chili powder, cumin, salt, and pepper until well coated.
3. Spread the seasoned sweet potatoes in a single layer on a baking sheet.
4. Roast in the preheated oven for 20-25 minutes or until the sweet potatoes are tender and slightly crispy, tossing halfway through.
5. While the sweet potatoes are roasting, warm the whole wheat tortillas in a dry skillet or microwave.
6. Heat the black beans in a saucepan over low heat.
7. Assemble the tacos by placing roasted sweet potatoes and black beans on each tortilla.
8. Garnish with salsa, avocado slices, and fresh cilantro if desired.
9. Serve these sweet potato and black bean tacos as a delicious and cholesterol-friendly meal.

Nutritional Facts (per serving, 2 tacos each): Calories: 340 | Total Fat: 9g | Saturated Fat: 1g | Cholesterol: 0mg | Sodium: 540mg | Total Carbohydrates: 58g | Dietary Fiber: 11g | Sugars: 6g | Protein: 10g

14. Cauliflower Rice Stir-Fry with Tofu

Introduction: Cauliflower Rice Stir-Fry with Tofu is a low-carb and cholesterol-friendly alternative to traditional stir-fry. Cauliflower rice replaces regular rice, and tofu adds plant-based protein to this flavorful dish.

Prep Time: 15 minutes | Cook Time: 20 minutes | Yield: 4 servings

Ingredients

- 1 head cauliflower, grated into rice-sized pieces (or store-bought cauliflower rice)
- 8 ounces firm tofu, cubed
- 2 tablespoons low-sodium soy sauce
- 2 tablespoons olive oil
- 1 onion, chopped
- 2 cloves garlic, minced
- 2 cups mixed vegetables (e.g., broccoli, bell peppers, snap peas, carrots)
- 1/4 cup low-sodium vegetable broth
- 1 teaspoon ginger, minced
- Salt and pepper to taste
- Sliced green onions and sesame seeds for garnish (optional)

Method of Preparation

1. In a bowl, marinate cubed tofu in low-sodium soy sauce for about 10 minutes.
2. In a large skillet or wok, heat olive oil over medium-high heat. Add chopped onion and sauté for 3-4 minutes until softened.
3. Add minced garlic, grated cauliflower, and mixed vegetables. Stir-fry for 5-7 minutes until vegetables are tender-crisp.
4. Push the vegetables to one side of the skillet and add the marinated tofu to the other side. Cook the tofu until it's browned on all sides.
5. Combine the tofu with the vegetables in the skillet.
6. Add low-sodium vegetable broth, minced ginger, salt, and pepper. Stir well.
7. Cook for an additional 2-3 minutes until everything is heated through.
8. Serve hot, garnished with sliced green onions and sesame seeds if desired.

Nutritional Facts (per serving): Calories: 190 | Total Fat: 11g | Saturated Fat: 1.5g | Cholesterol: 0mg | Sodium: 400mg | Total

Carbohydrates: 14g | Dietary Fiber: 6g | Sugars: 5g | Protein: 11g

- Zest and juice of 1 lemon
- 2 tablespoons fresh parsley, chopped
- 1 tablespoon fresh mint, chopped
- 2 tablespoons olive oil
- Salt and pepper to taste

15. Lemon Herb Couscous with Chickpeas and Olives

Introduction: Lemon Herb Couscous with Chickpeas and Olives is a zesty and Mediterranean-inspired dish that's rich in flavor and plant-based protein. It's a cholesterol-friendly option that's easy to prepare.

Prep Time: 10 minutes | Cook Time: 10 minutes | Yield: 4 servings

Ingredients:

- 1 cup whole wheat couscous
- 1 1/4 cups vegetable broth
- 1 can (15 ounces) chickpeas, drained and rinsed
- 1/2 cup Kalamata olives, pitted and sliced

Method of Preparation:

1. In a saucepan, bring the vegetable broth to a boil. Stir in the couscous, cover, and remove from heat. Let it sit for 5 minutes.
2. Fluff the cooked couscous with a fork.
3. In a large bowl, combine the cooked couscous, chickpeas, sliced Kalamata olives, lemon zest, lemon juice, fresh parsley, and fresh mint.
4. Drizzle with olive oil and toss to combine.
5. Season with salt and pepper to taste.
6. Serve this lemon herb couscous as a refreshing and cholesterol-friendly side dish or light meal.

Nutritional Facts (per serving): Calories: 330 | Total Fat: 10g | Saturated Fat: 1.5g | Cholesterol: 0mg | Sodium: 590mg | Total Carbohydrates: 51g | Dietary Fiber: 9g | Sugars: 3g | Protein: 11g

1. Grilled Chicken Breast with Lemon and Herbs

Introduction: Grilled Chicken Breast with Lemon and Herbs is a simple yet flavorful dish that's low in cholesterol and high in protein. The combination of zesty lemon and aromatic herbs makes this dish a delight for your taste buds.

Prep Time: 10 minutes | Cook Time: 15 minutes | Yield: 4 servings

Ingredients:

- 4 boneless, skinless chicken breasts
- Zest and juice of 1 lemon
- 2 cloves garlic, minced
- 2 tablespoons fresh herbs (e.g., rosemary, thyme, or oregano), chopped
- 2 tablespoons olive oil
- Salt and pepper to taste

Method of Preparation:

1. In a bowl, whisk together the lemon zest, lemon juice, minced garlic, fresh herbs, olive oil, salt, and pepper to create a marinade.
2. Place the chicken breasts in a resealable plastic bag and pour the marinade over them. Seal the bag and refrigerate for at least 30 minutes.
3. Preheat the grill to medium-high heat.
4. Remove the chicken breasts from the marinade and grill for about 6-7 minutes per side or until the internal temperature reaches 165°F (74°C) and the chicken is no longer pink.
5. Let the grilled chicken rest for a few minutes before serving.

Nutritional Facts (per serving): Calories: 220 | Total Fat: 10g | Saturated Fat: 2g | Cholesterol: 80mg | Sodium: 100mg | Total Carbohydrates: 1g | Dietary Fiber: 0g | Sugars: 0g | Protein: 30g

2. Turkey and Vegetable Stir-Fry with Ginger

Introduction: Turkey and Vegetable Stir-Fry with Ginger is a colorful and nutritious dish that's low in cholesterol and high in flavor. The addition of ginger adds a zesty kick to this stir-fry.

Prep Time: 15 minutes | Cook Time: 15 minutes | Yield: 4 servings

Ingredients

- 1 pound lean ground turkey
- 2 tablespoons low-sodium soy sauce
- 1 tablespoon fresh ginger, minced
- 2 cloves garlic, minced
- 2 cups broccoli florets
- 1 red bell pepper, sliced
- 1 carrot, thinly sliced
- 1 cup snap peas
- 2 tablespoons olive oil
- Salt and pepper to taste
- Cooked brown rice or quinoa for serving

Method of Preparation

1. In a small bowl, mix together the low-sodium soy sauce, minced ginger, and minced garlic. Set aside.
2. In a large skillet or wok, heat olive oil over medium-high heat.
3. Add the ground turkey and cook, breaking it apart with a spatula, until it's no longer pink.
4. Add the broccoli, red bell pepper, carrot, and snap peas to the skillet. Stir-fry for about 5-7 minutes until the vegetables are tender-crisp.
5. Pour the ginger-garlic sauce over the turkey and vegetables. Stir-fry for an additional 2-3 minutes.
6. Season with salt and pepper to taste.
7. Serve the turkey and vegetable stir-fry over cooked brown rice or quinoa.

Nutritional Facts (per serving, without rice or quinoa): Calories: 220 | Total Fat: 9g | Saturated Fat: 2g | Cholesterol: 55mg | Sodium: 420mg | Total Carbohydrates: 12g | Dietary Fiber: 3g | Sugars: 4g | Protein: 23g

3. Baked Salmon with Dill and Asparagus

Introduction: Baked Salmon with Dill and Asparagus is a heart-healthy dish packed with omega-3 fatty acids and fresh flavors. The combination of salmon and asparagus is a delicious and cholesterol-friendly choice.

Prep Time: 10 minutes | Cook Time: 15 minutes | Yield: 4 servings

Ingredients

- 4 salmon fillets
- 1 bunch asparagus, trimmed
- Zest and juice of 1 lemon
- 2 tablespoons fresh dill, chopped
- 2 cloves garlic, minced
- 2 tablespoons olive oil
- Salt and pepper to taste

Method of Preparation

1. Preheat the oven to 400°F (200°C).
2. In a bowl, whisk together the lemon zest, lemon juice, chopped fresh dill, minced garlic, olive oil, salt, and pepper to create a marinade.

3. Place the salmon fillets and trimmed asparagus in a baking dish. Pour the marinade over them.
4. Bake in the preheated oven for about 12-15 minutes or until the salmon flakes easily with a fork and the asparagus is tender.
5. Serve this baked salmon with dill and asparagus as a nutritious and cholesterol-friendly meal.

Nutritional Facts (per serving): Calories: 350 | Total Fat: 20g | Saturated Fat: 3.5g | Cholesterol: 80mg | Sodium: 200mg | Total Carbohydrates: 6g | Dietary Fiber: 2g | Sugars: 2g | Protein: 35g

4. Lean Beef and Broccoli Stir-Fry

Introduction: Lean Beef and Broccoli Stir-Fry is a savory and protein-packed dish that's low in cholesterol. The tender slices of beef and crisp broccoli are coated in a flavorful stir-fry sauce.

Prep Time: 15 minutes | Cook Time: 15 minutes | Yield: 4 servings

Ingredients

- 1 pound lean beef sirloin, thinly sliced
- 2 tablespoons low-sodium soy sauce
- 1 tablespoon oyster sauce
- 1 tablespoon fresh ginger, minced
- 2 cloves garlic, minced
- 4 cups broccoli florets
- 1 red bell pepper, sliced
- 2 tablespoons olive oil
- Cooked brown rice for serving

Method of Preparation

1. In a small bowl, combine the low-sodium soy sauce, oyster sauce, minced ginger, and minced garlic. Set aside.
2. In a large skillet or wok, heat olive oil over medium-high heat.
3. Add the thinly sliced beef and stir-fry for about 2-3 minutes until it's no longer pink. Remove it from the skillet and set aside.
4. In the same skillet, add the broccoli florets and red bell pepper. Stir-fry for about 5-7 minutes until the vegetables are tender-crisp.
5. Return the cooked beef to the skillet and pour the sauce over the beef and vegetables. Stir-fry for an additional 2-3 minutes.
6. Serve the lean beef and broccoli stir-fry over cooked brown rice.

Nutritional Facts (per serving, without rice): Calories: 250 | Total Fat: 10g | Saturated Fat: 2g | Cholesterol: 70mg | Sodium: 450mg | Total Carbohydrates: 12g | Dietary Fiber: 3g | Sugars: 4g | Protein: 28g

5. Turkey Burger with Avocado and Lettuce Wrap

Introduction: The Turkey Burger with Avocado and Lettuce Wrap is a delicious and cholesterol-friendly alternative to traditional burgers. The use of lettuce leaves as wraps keeps it low in carbs and calories while the creamy avocado adds richness.

Prep Time: 15 minutes | Cook Time: 12 minutes | Yield: 4 servings

Ingredients:

- 1 pound lean ground turkey
- 1/2 cup finely chopped red onion

- 2 cloves garlic, minced
- 1 teaspoon ground cumin
- 1 teaspoon chili powder
- Salt and pepper to taste
- 4 large lettuce leaves (e.g., iceberg or butter lettuce)
- 1 ripe avocado, sliced
- Sliced tomatoes and red onion for garnish (optional)

Method of Preparation:

1. In a bowl, combine the lean ground turkey, finely chopped red onion, minced garlic, ground cumin, chili powder, salt, and pepper. Mix well.
2. Divide the turkey mixture into four equal portions and shape them into burger patties.
3. Preheat a grill or grill pan over medium-high heat. Grill the turkey burgers for about 5-6 minutes per side, or until they reach an internal temperature of 165°F (74°C).
4. While the burgers are cooking, prepare the lettuce wraps by washing and drying the lettuce leaves.
5. Place each cooked turkey burger on a lettuce leaf.
6. Top with slices of ripe avocado and, if desired, sliced tomatoes and red onion.
7. Serve the turkey burger with avocado and lettuce wrap as a light and cholesterol-friendly meal.

Nutritional Facts (per serving): Calories: 220 | Total Fat: 11g | Saturated Fat: 2g | Cholesterol: 60mg | Sodium: 260mg | Total Carbohydrates: 7g | Dietary Fiber: 4g | Sugars: 2g | Protein: 23g

6. Lemon Garlic Shrimp Skewers

Introduction: Lemon Garlic Shrimp Skewers are a light and zesty dish that's high in protein and low in cholesterol. Grilled to perfection, these shrimp skewers are bursting with citrus and garlic flavors.

Prep Time: 15 minutes | Cook Time: 6 minutes | Yield: 4 servings

Ingredients:

- 1 pound large shrimp, peeled and deveined
- Zest and juice of 1 lemon
- 2 cloves garlic, minced
- 2 tablespoons fresh parsley, chopped
- 2 tablespoons olive oil
- Salt and pepper to taste
- Wooden skewers, soaked in water

Method of Preparation:

1. In a bowl, whisk together the lemon zest, lemon juice, minced garlic, chopped fresh parsley, olive oil, salt, and pepper to create a marinade.
2. Thread the peeled and deveined shrimp onto the soaked wooden skewers.
3. Brush the shrimp skewers with the marinade, ensuring they are well-coated.
4. Preheat the grill to medium-high heat.
5. Grill the shrimp skewers for about 2-3 minutes per side or until they turn pink and opaque.
6. Serve these lemon garlic shrimp skewers as a delightful and cholesterol-friendly appetizer or main dish.

Nutritional Facts (per serving): Calories: 140 | Total Fat: 6g | Saturated Fat: 1g | Cholesterol: 170mg | Sodium: 180mg | Total Carbohydrates: 3g | Dietary Fiber: 0g | Sugars: 0g | Protein: 18g

7. Pork Tenderloin with Apple Cider Glaze

Introduction: Pork Tenderloin with Apple Cider Glaze is a savory-sweet dish that's low in cholesterol. The tender pork is paired with a flavorful apple cider glaze for a delightful combination of tastes.

Prep Time: 15 minutes | Cook Time: 25 minutes | Yield: 4 servings

Ingredients:

- 1 pound pork tenderloin
- 1 cup apple cider
- 2 tablespoons balsamic vinegar
- 2 cloves garlic, minced
- 1 teaspoon dried thyme
- Salt and pepper to taste
- 1 tablespoon olive oil

Method of Preparation:

1. Preheat the oven to 400°F (200°C).
2. Season the pork tenderloin with salt, pepper, and dried thyme.
3. In an ovenproof skillet, heat olive oil over medium-high heat. Add the pork tenderloin and sear for 2-3 minutes on each side until browned.
4. Transfer the skillet to the preheated oven and roast for about 15-20 minutes or until the internal temperature of the pork reaches 145°F (63°C).
5. While the pork is roasting, make the apple cider glaze. In a small saucepan, combine the apple cider, balsamic vinegar, minced garlic, salt, and pepper. Simmer over medium heat for about 10-15 minutes until the glaze thickens.
6. Once the pork is cooked, let it rest for a few minutes before slicing.
7. Drizzle the apple cider glaze over the sliced pork tenderloin before serving.

Nutritional Facts (per serving): Calories: 230 | Total Fat: 6g | Saturated Fat: 1.5g | Cholesterol: 75mg | Sodium: 70mg | Total Carbohydrates: 13g | Dietary Fiber: 0g | Sugars: 9g | Protein: 28g

8. Baked Chicken Thighs with Brussels Sprouts

Introduction: Baked Chicken Thighs with Brussels Sprouts is a one-pan meal that's hearty and low in cholesterol. The combination of tender chicken thighs and roasted Brussels sprouts is both delicious and nutritious.

Prep Time: 15 minutes | Cook Time: 30 minutes | Yield: 4 servings

Ingredients:

- 4 bone-in, skinless chicken thighs
- 1 pound Brussels sprouts, trimmed and halved
- 2 tablespoons olive oil
- 2 cloves garlic, minced
- 1 teaspoon dried thyme
- Salt and pepper to taste
- Lemon wedges for garnish (optional)

Method of Preparation:

1. Preheat the oven to 425°F (220°C).
2. In a large bowl, combine the trimmed and halved Brussels sprouts, olive oil, minced garlic, dried thyme, salt, and pepper. Toss to coat.

3. Place the chicken thighs and seasoned Brussels sprouts on a baking sheet or in an ovenproof skillet.
4. Bake in the preheated oven for about 25-30 minutes or until the chicken thighs are cooked through and the Brussels sprouts are tender and caramelized.
5. Serve the baked chicken thighs with Brussels sprouts as a wholesome and cholesterol-friendly meal, garnished with lemon wedges if desired.

Nutritional Facts (per serving): Calories: 320 | Total Fat: 18g | Saturated Fat: 4g Cholesterol: 125mg | Sodium: 140mg | Total Carbohydrates: 11g | Dietary Fiber: 4g | Sugars: 3g | Protein: 30g

9. Ground Chicken Lettuce Wraps with Asian Sauce

Introduction: Ground Chicken Lettuce Wraps with Asian Sauce are a light and flavorful dish that's low in cholesterol and carbs. The juicy ground chicken is seasoned with a savory Asian-inspired sauce, perfect for wrapping in lettuce leaves.

Prep Time: 15 minutes | Cook Time: 15 minutes | Yield: 4 servings

Ingredients:

- 1 pound ground chicken
- 2 tablespoons low-sodium soy sauce
- 1 tablespoon rice vinegar
- 1 teaspoon sesame oil
- 2 cloves garlic, minced
- 1 teaspoon fresh ginger, minced
- 1 cup water chestnuts, chopped
- 1/4 cup green onions, chopped

- 1 head iceberg or butter lettuce, leaves separated

Method of Preparation:

1. In a small bowl, whisk together the low-sodium soy sauce, rice vinegar, sesame oil, minced garlic, and minced ginger. Set aside.
2. In a large skillet, cook the ground chicken over medium-high heat until it's no longer pink, breaking it apart with a spatula.
3. Stir in the chopped water chestnuts and green onions and cook for an additional 2-3 minutes.
4. Pour the Asian sauce over the cooked chicken mixture and stir to combine. Cook for another 2-3 minutes.
5. To serve, spoon the ground chicken mixture into individual lettuce leaves, creating wraps.
6. Enjoy these ground chicken lettuce wraps with Asian sauce as a light and cholesterol-friendly meal.

Nutritional Facts (per serving): Calories: 220 | Total Fat: 10g | Saturated Fat: 2g | Cholesterol: 85mg | Sodium: 530mg | Total Carbohydrates: 9g | Dietary Fiber: 2g | Sugars: 3g | Protein: 22g

10. Baked Cod with Tomato and Olive Relish

Introduction: Baked Cod with Tomato and Olive Relish is a light and Mediterranean-inspired dish that's rich in flavor and low in cholesterol. The flaky cod is topped with a zesty tomato and olive relish.

Prep Time: 15 minutes | Cook Time: 15 minutes | Yield: 4 servings

Ingredients:

- 4 cod fillets
- 2 cups cherry tomatoes, halved
- 1/2 cup Kalamata olives, pitted and chopped
- 2 cloves garlic, minced
- Zest and juice of 1 lemon
- 2 tablespoons fresh basil, chopped
- 2 tablespoons olive oil
- Salt and pepper to taste

Method of Preparation:

1. Preheat the oven to 400°F (200°C).
2. In a bowl, combine the halved cherry tomatoes, chopped Kalamata olives, minced garlic, lemon zest, lemon juice, chopped fresh basil, olive oil, salt, and pepper. Mix to make the tomato and olive relish.
3. Place the cod fillets on a baking sheet lined with parchment paper.
4. Spoon the tomato and olive relish over the cod fillets.
5. Bake in the preheated oven for about 12-15 minutes or until the cod flakes easily with a fork and the relish is bubbly.
6. Serve this baked cod with tomato and olive relish as a light and cholesterol-friendly dish.

Nutritional Facts (per serving): Calories: 220 | Total Fat: 9g | Saturated Fat: 1g | Cholesterol: 55mg | Sodium: 620mg | Total Carbohydrates: 9g | Dietary Fiber: 2g | Sugars: 4g | Protein: 27g

11. Turkey Meatballs with Zucchini Noodles

Introduction: Turkey Meatballs with Zucchini Noodles is a lighter and lower-cholesterol twist on traditional spaghetti and meatballs. The turkey meatballs are paired with spiralized zucchini noodles and a flavorful tomato sauce.

Prep Time: 20 minutes | Cook Time: 25 minutes | Yield: 4 servings

Ingredients:

For Turkey Meatballs:

- 1 pound ground turkey
- 1/4 cup whole wheat breadcrumbs
- 1/4 cup grated Parmesan cheese
- 1/4 cup fresh parsley, chopped
- 1 egg
- 2 cloves garlic, minced
- Salt and pepper to taste

For Tomato Sauce:

- 1 can (14 ounces) crushed tomatoes
- 2 cloves garlic, minced
- 1 teaspoon dried basil
- 1 teaspoon dried oregano
- Salt and pepper to taste

For Zucchini Noodles:

- 4 medium zucchinis, spiralized into noodles
- 1 tablespoon olive oil

Method of Preparation

For Turkey Meatballs:

1. In a bowl, combine the ground turkey, whole wheat breadcrumbs, grated Parmesan cheese, chopped fresh parsley, egg, minced garlic, salt, and pepper. Mix well.
2. Form the mixture into meatballs, about 1 to 1.5 inches in diameter.
3. In a large skillet, heat olive oil over medium-high heat. Cook the meatballs for about 8-10 minutes, turning occasionally until they are browned and cooked through.

For Tomato Sauce:

4. In a separate saucepan, combine the crushed tomatoes, minced garlic, dried basil, dried oregano, salt, and pepper. Simmer over low heat for about 10-15 minutes.

For Zucchini Noodles:

5. Spiralize the zucchinis into noodles.
6. Heat olive oil in a separate pan and sauté the zucchini noodles for about 2-3 minutes until they are tender.
7. Serve the turkey meatballs over the zucchini noodles with a spoonful of tomato sauce.

Nutritional Facts (per serving): Calories: 320 | Total Fat: 14g | Saturated Fat: 4g | Cholesterol: 115mg | Sodium: 520mg | Total Carbohydrates: 18g | Dietary Fiber: 4g | Sugars: 8g | Protein: 30g

12. Tofu and Vegetable Stir-Fry with Sesame

Introduction: Tofu and Vegetable Stir-Fry with Sesame is a nutritious and cholesterol-friendly vegetarian dish. It combines tofu, colorful vegetables, and a savory sesame sauce for a delightful stir-fry.

Prep Time: 20 minutes | Cook Time: 15 minutes | Yield: 4 servings

Ingredients:

- 1 block (14 ounces) firm tofu, cubed
- 2 tablespoons low-sodium soy sauce
- 1 tablespoon sesame oil
- 2 cloves garlic, minced
- 1 teaspoon fresh ginger, minced
- 4 cups mixed vegetables (e.g., broccoli, bell peppers, snap peas, carrots), chopped
- 2 tablespoons sesame seeds
- Cooked brown rice or quinoa for serving

Method of Preparation:

1. In a bowl, combine the cubed tofu, low-sodium soy sauce, sesame oil, minced garlic, and minced ginger. Toss to coat and marinate for 10-15 minutes.
2. Heat a large skillet or wok over medium-high heat. Add the marinated tofu and stir-fry for about 5-7 minutes until it's browned and slightly crispy. Remove from the skillet and set aside.
3. In the same skillet, add the chopped mixed vegetables and stir-fry for about 5 minutes until they are tender-crisp.
4. Return the cooked tofu to the skillet with the vegetables and toss to combine.
5. Sprinkle sesame seeds over the stir-fry and cook for an additional 2-3 minutes.
6. Serve the tofu and vegetable stir-fry with sesame over cooked brown rice or quinoa.

Nutritional Facts (per serving, without rice or quinoa): Calories: 180 | Total Fat: 12g | Saturated Fat: 2g | Cholesterol: 0mg | Sodium: 420mg | Total Carbohydrates: 12g | Dietary Fiber: 4g | Sugars: 4g | Protein: 12g

13. Grilled Portobello Mushrooms with Balsamic Glaze

Introduction: Grilled Portobello Mushrooms with Balsamic Glaze is a satisfying and cholesterol-friendly vegetarian dish. The meaty Portobello mushrooms are marinated and grilled to perfection, then drizzled with a sweet and tangy balsamic glaze.

Prep Time: 15 minutes | Cook Time: 10 minutes | Yield: 4 servings

Ingredients:

- 4 large Portobello mushrooms, stems removed
- 1/4 cup balsamic vinegar
- 2 tablespoons olive oil
- 2 cloves garlic, minced
- 1 teaspoon dried rosemary
- Salt and pepper to taste
- Fresh parsley for garnish (optional)

For Balsamic Glaze:

- 1/2 cup balsamic vinegar
- 2 tablespoons honey (or maple syrup for a vegan option)

Method of Preparation

For Marinated Mushrooms:

1. In a bowl, whisk together the balsamic vinegar, olive oil, minced garlic, dried rosemary, salt, and pepper.
2. Brush the Portobello mushrooms with the marinade on both sides and let them marinate for about 10 minutes.
3. Preheat the grill to medium-high heat.
4. Grill the mushrooms for about 4-5 minutes per side until they are tender and have grill marks.

For Balsamic Glaze:

5. While the mushrooms are grilling, prepare the balsamic glaze. In a small saucepan, combine the balsamic vinegar and honey (or maple syrup). Simmer over low heat for about 5-7 minutes until it thickens.
6. Serve the grilled Portobello mushrooms with a drizzle of balsamic glaze and garnish with fresh parsley if desired.

Nutritional Facts (per serving): Calories: 110 | Total Fat: 6g | Saturated Fat: 1g | Cholesterol: 0mg | Sodium: 15mg | Total Carbohydrates: 11g | Dietary Fiber: 1g | Sugars: 7g | Protein: 3g

14. Baked Trout with Almonds and Lemon Butter

Introduction: Baked Trout with Almonds and Lemon Butter is a light and heart-healthy dish that's low in cholesterol. The delicate trout fillets are topped with toasted almonds and a zesty lemon butter sauce.

Prep Time: 15 minutes | Cook Time: 15 minutes | Yield: 4 servings

Ingredients

- 4 trout fillets
- 1/2 cup sliced almonds, toasted
- Zest and juice of 1 lemon
- 2 tablespoons fresh parsley, chopped
- 4 tablespoons unsalted butter
- Salt and pepper to taste

Method of Preparation:

1. Preheat the oven to 375°F (190°C).
2. Season the trout fillets with salt and pepper and place them on a baking sheet lined with parchment paper.
3. Bake the trout fillets in the preheated oven for about 12-15 minutes or until they are cooked through and flake easily with a fork.
4. While the trout is baking, prepare the lemon butter sauce. In a saucepan, melt the unsalted butter over low heat. Stir in the lemon zest, lemon juice, and chopped fresh parsley.
5. Toast the sliced almonds in a dry skillet over medium heat until they are golden brown.
6. Once the trout is done baking, top each fillet with toasted almonds and drizzle with lemon butter sauce.

Nutritional Facts (per serving): Calories: 280 | Total Fat: 21g | Saturated Fat: 8g | Cholesterol:

85mg | Sodium: 60mg | Total Carbohydrates: 3g | Dietary Fiber: 2g | Sugars: 1g | Protein: 20g

15. Turkey and Quinoa Stuffed Bell Peppers

Introduction: Turkey and Quinoa Stuffed Bell Peppers are a wholesome and cholesterol-friendly meal. Bell peppers are filled with a flavorful mixture of ground turkey, quinoa, vegetables, and herbs.

Prep Time: 20 minutes | Cook Time: 40 minutes | Yield: 4 servings

Ingredients:

- 4 large bell peppers, any color
- 1 pound lean ground turkey
- 1 cup quinoa, cooked
- 1 cup diced tomatoes
- 1/2 cup black beans, drained and rinsed
- 1/2 cup corn kernels (fresh or frozen)
- 1/4 cup diced red onion
- 2 cloves garlic, minced
- 1 teaspoon chili powder
- 1 teaspoon ground cumin
- Salt and pepper to taste
- 1 cup low-sodium vegetable broth
- 1/2 cup shredded low-fat cheese (optional)

Method of Preparation

1. Preheat the oven to 350°F (175°C).
2. Cut the tops off the bell peppers and remove the seeds and membranes. Set aside.
3. In a large skillet, cook the lean ground turkey over medium-high heat until it's no longer pink, breaking it apart with a spatula. Drain any excess fat.
4. In a mixing bowl, combine the cooked ground turkey, cooked quinoa, diced tomatoes, black beans, corn, diced red onion, minced garlic, chili powder, ground cumin, salt, and pepper. Mix well.
5. Stuff each bell pepper with the turkey and quinoa mixture.
6. Place the stuffed bell peppers in a baking dish and pour the low-sodium vegetable broth into the dish.
7. Cover the dish with aluminum foil and bake in the preheated oven for about 30-35 minutes or until the peppers are tender.
8. If desired, top each stuffed bell pepper with shredded low-fat cheese and return to the oven for an additional 5 minutes or until the cheese is melted and bubbly.

Nutritional Facts (per serving, without cheese): Calories: 350 | Total Fat: 4g | Saturated Fat: 1g | Cholesterol: 55mg | Sodium: 390mg | Total Carbohydrates: 48g | Dietary Fiber: 8g | Sugars: 7g | Protein: 33g

FISH AND SEAFOOD

1. Grilled Tuna Steak with Mango Salsa

Introduction: Grilled Tuna Steak with Mango Salsa is a flavorful and heart-healthy dish. The grilled tuna steak is paired with a vibrant mango salsa for a burst of tropical flavors.

Prep Time: 15 minutes | Cook Time: 10 minutes | Yield: 4 servings

Ingredients:

For Grilled Tuna Steak:

- 4 tuna steaks (6 ounces each)
- 2 tablespoons olive oil
- 1 teaspoon paprika
- Salt and pepper to taste

For Mango Salsa:

- 2 ripe mangoes, diced

- 1/2 red onion, finely chopped
- 1 red bell pepper, diced
- 1/4 cup fresh cilantro, chopped
- Juice of 1 lime
- Salt and pepper to taste

Method of Preparation

For Grilled Tuna Steak:

1. Preheat the grill to medium-high heat.
2. Brush the tuna steaks with olive oil and season with paprika, salt, and pepper.
3. Grill the tuna steaks for about 3-4 minutes per side for medium-rare or longer for desired doneness.

For Mango Salsa:

4. In a bowl, combine the diced mangoes, chopped red onion, diced red bell pepper, chopped fresh cilantro, lime juice, salt, and pepper. Mix well.

5. Serve the grilled tuna steaks with a generous spoonful of mango salsa.

Nutritional Facts (per serving): Calories: 320 | Total Fat: 9g | Saturated Fat: 1g | Cholesterol: 65mg | Sodium: 180mg | Total Carbohydrates: 30g | Dietary Fiber: 4g | Sugars: 23g | Protein: 30g

2. Baked Cod with Herbed Crust

Introduction: Baked Cod with Herbed Crust is a light and cholesterol-friendly dish. The cod fillets are coated with a flavorful herb crust and baked to perfection.

Prep Time: 15 minutes | Cook Time: 15 minutes | Yield: 4 servings

Ingredients

- 4 cod fillets
- 1/2 cup whole wheat breadcrumbs
- 2 tablespoons fresh parsley, chopped
- 2 tablespoons fresh dill, chopped
- 2 cloves garlic, minced
- Zest of 1 lemon
- 2 tablespoons olive oil
- Salt and pepper to taste
- Lemon wedges for garnish (optional)

Method of Preparation

1. Preheat the oven to 400°F (200°C).
2. In a bowl, combine the whole wheat breadcrumbs, chopped fresh parsley, chopped fresh dill, minced garlic, lemon zest, olive oil, salt, and pepper. Mix well to create the herb crust.
3. Place the cod fillets on a baking sheet lined with parchment paper.
4. Press the herb crust mixture onto the top of each cod fillet.

5. Bake in the preheated oven for about 12-15 minutes or until the cod flakes easily with a fork and the crust is golden brown.
6. Garnish with lemon wedges if desired before serving.

Nutritional Facts (per serving): Calories: 220 | Total Fat: 9g | Saturated Fat: 1.5g | Cholesterol: 60mg | Sodium: 220mg | Total Carbohydrates: 9g | Dietary Fiber: 1g | Sugars: 1g | Protein: 25g

3. Garlic Butter Shrimp and Broccoli

Introduction: Garlic Butter Shrimp and Broccoli is a quick and flavorful dish that's low in cholesterol. Succulent shrimp are sautéed with garlic and served with tender broccoli in a delicious buttery sauce.

Prep Time: 10 minutes | Cook Time: 15 minutes | Yield: 4 servings

Ingredients

- 1 pound large shrimp, peeled and deveined
- 2 cups broccoli florets
- 4 cloves garlic, minced
- 2 tablespoons unsalted butter
- 2 tablespoons olive oil
- Juice of 1 lemon
- Salt and pepper to taste
- Fresh parsley for garnish (optional)

Method of Preparation

1. In a large skillet, heat the olive oil and 1 tablespoon of butter over medium-high heat.
2. Add the minced garlic and sauté for about 1 minute until fragrant.

3. Add the shrimp to the skillet and cook for 2-3 minutes per side until they turn pink and opaque. Remove the cooked shrimp from the skillet and set them aside.
4. In the same skillet, add the broccoli florets and sauté for about 5-7 minutes until they are tender.
5. Return the cooked shrimp to the skillet with the broccoli.
6. Add the remaining 1 tablespoon of butter and lemon juice to the skillet. Stir to coat the shrimp and broccoli with the garlic butter sauce.
7. Season with salt and pepper, and garnish with fresh parsley if desired.

Nutritional Facts (per serving): Calories: 240 | Total Fat: 15g | Saturated Fat: 5g | Cholesterol: 175mg | Sodium: 250mg | Total Carbohydrates: 5g | Dietary Fiber: 2g | Sugars: 1g | Protein: 21g

4. Seared Scallops with Spinach and Lemon

Introduction: Seared Scallops with Spinach and Lemon is an elegant and cholesterol-friendly seafood dish. Tender scallops are seared to perfection and served over a bed of sautéed spinach with a zesty lemon sauce.

Prep Time: 10 minutes | Cook Time: 10 minutes | Yield: 4 servings

Ingredients

- 1 pound sea scallops
- 2 tablespoons olive oil
- 4 cups fresh spinach
- 2 cloves garlic, minced
- Zest and juice of 1 lemon
- Salt and pepper to taste

- Fresh parsley for garnish (optional)

Method of Preparation:

1. Pat the scallops dry with paper towels and season with salt and pepper.
2. In a large skillet, heat the olive oil over medium-high heat.
3. Add the scallops to the skillet and sear for about 2-3 minutes per side until they are golden brown and cooked through. Remove the cooked scallops from the skillet and set them aside.
4. In the same skillet, add minced garlic and sauté for about 1 minute until fragrant.
5. Add the fresh spinach to the skillet and cook for about 2-3 minutes until it wilts.
6. Return the seared scallops to the skillet.
7. Add the lemon zest and lemon juice to the skillet and toss to coat the scallops and spinach with the lemon sauce.
8. Garnish with fresh parsley if desired before serving.

Nutritional Facts (per serving): Calories: 180 | Total Fat: 7g | Saturated Fat: 1g | Cholesterol: 45mg | Sodium: 450mg | Total Carbohydrates: 8g | Dietary Fiber: 3g | Sugars: 1g | Protein: 20g

5. Miso Glazed Salmon with Bok Choy

Introduction: Miso Glazed Salmon with Bok Choy is a delightful and heart-healthy dish. Salmon fillets are coated with a savory miso glaze and served with steamed bok choy for a balanced meal.

Prep Time: 15 minutes | Cook Time: 15 minutes | Yield: 4 servings

Ingredients:

For Miso Glazed Salmon:

- 4 salmon fillets (6 ounces each)
- 2 tablespoons white miso paste
- 2 tablespoons honey
- 1 tablespoon low-sodium soy sauce
- 1 tablespoon rice vinegar
- 2 cloves garlic, minced
- 1 teaspoon grated fresh ginger
- Sesame seeds for garnish (optional)

For Steamed Bok Choy:

- 4 baby bok choy heads, halved
- 1 tablespoon sesame oil
- Salt and pepper to taste

Method of Preparation

For Miso Glazed Salmon:

1. Preheat the oven to 375°F (190°C).
2. In a bowl, whisk together the white miso paste, honey, low-sodium soy sauce, rice vinegar, minced garlic, and grated fresh ginger to create the miso glaze.
3. Place the salmon fillets on a baking sheet lined with parchment paper.
4. Brush the salmon fillets generously with the miso glaze.
5. Bake in the preheated oven for about 12-15 minutes or until the salmon flakes easily with a fork and the glaze is caramelized.
6. Garnish with sesame seeds if desired.

For Steamed Bok Choy:

7. While the salmon is baking, steam the halved baby bok choy heads for about 4-5 minutes until they are tender.
8. Drizzle sesame oil over the steamed bok choy and season with salt and pepper.

Nutritional Facts (per serving): Calories: 320 | Total Fat: 13g | Saturated Fat: 2g | Cholesterol: 65mg | Sodium: 500mg | Total Carbohydrates:

21g | Dietary Fiber: 2g | Sugars: 15g | Protein: 28g

6. Lemon Garlic Tilapia Fillets

Introduction: Lemon Garlic Tilapia Fillets is a simple and cholesterol-friendly dish. Tilapia fillets are infused with zesty lemon and garlic flavors and pan-seared for a quick and delicious meal.

Prep Time: 10 minutes | Cook Time: 10 minutes | Yield: 4 servings

Ingredients

- 4 tilapia fillets
- 2 tablespoons olive oil
- 4 cloves garlic, minced
- Zest and juice of 1 lemon
- Salt and pepper to taste
- Fresh parsley for garnish (optional)

Method of Preparation:

1. Season the tilapia fillets with salt and pepper.
2. In a large skillet, heat the olive oil over medium-high heat.
3. Add the minced garlic to the skillet and sauté for about 1 minute until fragrant.
4. Place the tilapia fillets in the skillet and cook for about 3-4 minutes per side until they are cooked through and golden brown.
5. Drizzle the lemon juice and lemon zest over the tilapia fillets.
6. Garnish with fresh parsley if desired before serving.

Nutritional Facts (per serving): Calories: 160 | Total Fat: 7g | Saturated Fat: 1g | Cholesterol:

45mg | Sodium: 110mg | Total Carbohydrates: 2g | Dietary Fiber: 0g | Sugars: 0g | Protein: 23g

7. Cilantro Lime Grilled Swordfish

Introduction: Cilantro Lime Grilled Swordfish is a zesty and heart-healthy dish. Swordfish steaks are marinated in a cilantro lime sauce and grilled to perfection, making it a delightful meal.

Prep Time: 15 minutes | Marinating Time: 30 minutes | Cook Time: 10 minutes | Yield: 4 servings

Ingredients

- 4 swordfish steaks
- 1/4 cup fresh cilantro, chopped
- Juice and zest of 2 limes
- 2 cloves garlic, minced
- 2 tablespoons olive oil
- Salt and pepper to taste
- Lime wedges for garnish (optional)

Method of Preparation

1. In a bowl, combine the chopped cilantro, lime juice, lime zest, minced garlic, olive oil, salt, and pepper to create the cilantro lime marinade.
2. Place the swordfish steaks in a shallow dish and pour the marinade over them. Cover and refrigerate for at least 30 minutes to allow the flavors to infuse.
3. Preheat the grill to medium-high heat.
4. Remove the swordfish steaks from the marinade and grill for about 4-5 minutes per side or until they are cooked through and have grill marks.

5. Garnish with lime wedges if desired before serving.

Nutritional Facts (per serving): Calories: 270 | Total Fat: 12g | Saturated Fat: 2g | Cholesterol: 75mg | Sodium: 120mg | Total Carbohydrates: 2g | Dietary Fiber: 0g | Sugars: 0g | Protein: 38g

8. Poached Halibut with Caper and Lemon Sauce

Introduction: Poached Halibut with Caper and Lemon Sauce is a delicate and cholesterol-friendly seafood dish. Halibut fillets are poached to perfection and served with a tangy caper and lemon sauce.

Prep Time: 10 minutes | Cook Time: 15 minutes | Yield: 4 servings

Ingredients

For Poached Halibut:

- 4 halibut fillets (6 ounces each)
- 2 cups vegetable broth (low-sodium)
- 1/2 cup dry white wine (optional)
- 1 lemon, sliced
- 2 bay leaves
- Salt and pepper to taste

For Caper and Lemon Sauce:

- 2 tablespoons unsalted butter
- 2 tablespoons capers, drained
- Juice of 1 lemon
- Fresh parsley for garnish (optional)

Method of Preparation:

For Poached Halibut:

1. In a large skillet or shallow pan, combine the vegetable broth, dry white wine (if

59

using), lemon slices, bay leaves, salt, and pepper.

2. Bring the liquid to a gentle simmer over medium heat.
3. Add the halibut fillets to the simmering liquid and poach for about 5-7 minutes until they are opaque and cooked through. The exact cooking time may vary depending on the thickness of the fillets.
4. Using a slotted spatula, carefully remove the poached halibut fillets from the liquid and place them on serving plates.

For Caper and Lemon Sauce:

5. In a small saucepan, melt the unsalted butter over low heat.
6. Stir in the capers and lemon juice. Simmer for about 2-3 minutes until heated through.
7. Pour the caper and lemon sauce over the poached halibut fillets.
8. Garnish with fresh parsley if desired before serving.

Nutritional Facts (per serving): Calories: 220 | Total Fat: 9g | Saturated Fat: 4g | Cholesterol: 80mg | Sodium: 400mg | Total Carbohydrates: 6g | Dietary Fiber: 1g | Sugars: 1g | Protein: 28g

9. Spicy Sriracha Shrimp with Brown Rice

Introduction: Spicy Sriracha Shrimp with Brown Rice is a bold and heart-healthy dish. Succulent shrimp are coated in a spicy Sriracha sauce and served over wholesome brown rice.

Prep Time: 15 minutes | Cook Time: 20 minutes | Yield: 4 servings

Ingredients

For Spicy Sriracha Shrimp:

- 1 pound large shrimp, peeled and deveined
- 2 tablespoons Sriracha sauce (adjust to taste)
- 2 tablespoons low-sodium soy sauce
- 1 tablespoon honey
- 1 tablespoon olive oil
- 2 cloves garlic, minced
- 1 teaspoon grated fresh ginger
- Red pepper flakes (optional, for extra heat)
- Green onions for garnish (optional)

For Brown Rice:

- 1 cup brown rice
- 2 cups water
- Salt to taste

Method of Preparation

For Spicy Sriracha Shrimp:

1. In a bowl, whisk together the Sriracha sauce, low-sodium soy sauce, honey, minced garlic, grated fresh ginger, and red pepper flakes (if using).
2. In a large skillet, heat the olive oil over medium-high heat.
3. Add the shrimp to the skillet and cook for about 1-2 minutes per side until they start to turn pink.
4. Pour the Sriracha sauce mixture over the shrimp and cook for an additional 2-3 minutes until the shrimp are cooked through and the sauce thickens.
5. Garnish with sliced green onions if desired.

For Brown Rice:

6. In a separate pot, combine the brown rice, water, and a pinch of salt. Bring to a boil, then reduce the heat to low, cover, and simmer for about 15-20 minutes until the rice is tender and the water is absorbed.

Nutritional Facts (per serving): Calories: 320 | Total Fat: 5g | Saturated Fat: 1g | Cholesterol: 175mg | Sodium: 600mg | Total Carbohydrates: 47g | Dietary Fiber: 2g | Sugars: 5g | Protein: 21g

10. Tandoori Spiced Trout with Mint Raita

Introduction: Tandoori Spiced Trout with Mint Raita is a fragrant and cholesterol-friendly dish. Trout fillets are marinated in tandoori spices and served with a refreshing mint raita.

Prep Time: 15 minutes | Marinating Time: 30 minutes | Cook Time: 10 minutes | Yield: 4 servings

Ingredients

For Tandoori Spiced Trout

- 4 trout fillets
- 1/2 cup plain Greek yogurt
- 2 tablespoons tandoori spice blend
- 1 tablespoon olive oil
- Juice of 1 lemon
- Salt and pepper to taste

For Mint Raita:

- 1 cup plain Greek yogurt
- 1/4 cup fresh mint leaves, chopped
- 1/4 cucumber, grated
- 1 clove garlic, minced
- Salt and pepper to taste

Method of Preparation

For Tandoori Spiced Trout:

1. In a bowl, combine the plain Greek yogurt, tandoori spice blend, olive oil, lemon juice,

salt, and pepper to create the tandoori marinade.
2. Place the trout fillets in a shallow dish and pour the marinade over them. Cover and refrigerate for at least 30 minutes to allow the flavors to meld.
3. Preheat the grill to medium-high heat.
4. Remove the trout fillets from the marinade and grill for about 4-5 minutes per side until they are cooked through and have grill marks.

For Mint Raita:

5. In a bowl, combine the plain Greek yogurt, chopped fresh mint leaves, grated cucumber, minced garlic, salt, and pepper. Mix well to create the mint raita.
6. Serve the tandoori spiced trout with a dollop of mint raita.

Nutritional Facts (per serving): Calories: 280 | Total Fat: 10g | Saturated Fat: 3g | Cholesterol: 70mg | Sodium: 450mg | Total Carbohydrates: 11g | Dietary Fiber: 1g | Sugars: 6g | Protein: 35g

11. Herb-Crusted Mahi-Mahi with Quinoa

Introduction: Herb-Crusted Mahi-Mahi with Quinoa is a flavorful and heart-healthy dish. Mahi-Mahi fillets are coated in a fragrant herb crust and served with protein-rich quinoa.

Prep Time: 15 minutes | Cook Time: 20 minutes | Yield: 4 servings

Ingredients:

For Herb-Crusted Mahi-Mahi:

- 4 mahi-mahi fillets
- 1/2 cup whole wheat breadcrumbs
- 2 tablespoons fresh parsley, chopped
- 2 tablespoons fresh thyme, chopped
- 2 cloves garlic, minced
- Zest of 1 lemon
- 2 tablespoons olive oil
- Salt and pepper to taste

For Quinoa:

- 1 cup quinoa
- 2 cups vegetable broth (low-sodium)
- Salt and pepper to taste

Method of Preparation

For Herb-Crusted Mahi-Mahi:

1. Preheat the oven to 375°F (190°C).
2. In a bowl, combine the whole wheat breadcrumbs, chopped fresh parsley, chopped fresh thyme, minced garlic, lemon zest, olive oil, salt, and pepper to create the herb crust.
3. Place the mahi-mahi fillets on a baking sheet lined with parchment paper.
4. Press the herb crust mixture onto the top of each mahi-mahi fillet.
5. Bake in the preheated oven for about 12-15 minutes or until the fish flakes easily with a fork and the crust is golden brown.

For Quinoa:

6. In a saucepan, combine the quinoa and vegetable broth. Bring to a boil, then reduce the heat to low, cover, and simmer for about 15-20 minutes until the quinoa is tender and the liquid is absorbed.
7. Fluff the cooked quinoa with a fork and season with salt and pepper.

Nutritional Facts (per serving): Calories: 340 | Total Fat: 9g | Saturated Fat: 1g | Cholesterol: 125mg | Sodium: 250mg | Total Carbohydrates: 33g | Dietary Fiber: 4g | Sugars: 1g | Protein: 35g

12. Coconut-Curry Shrimp with Vegetables

Introduction: Coconut-Curry Shrimp with Vegetables is a vibrant and heart-healthy dish. Succulent shrimp are cooked in a creamy coconut-curry sauce with an array of colorful vegetables.

Prep Time: 15 minutes | Cook Time: 20 minutes | Yield: 4 servings

Ingredients:

- 1 pound large shrimp, peeled and deveined
- 1 can (14 ounces) coconut milk
- 2 tablespoons red curry paste
- 2 tablespoons fish sauce
- 1 tablespoon brown sugar
- 2 cups mixed vegetables (bell peppers, broccoli, carrots, etc.)
- 2 tablespoons vegetable oil
- Cooked brown rice for serving

Method of Preparation:

1. In a large skillet, heat the vegetable oil over medium-high heat.
2. Add the red curry paste to the skillet and stir-fry for about 1-2 minutes until fragrant.
3. Pour in the coconut milk and stir to combine with the curry paste.
4. Add the fish sauce and brown sugar to the skillet. Stir well to incorporate.
5. Add the mixed vegetables to the coconut-curry sauce and cook for about 5-7 minutes until they are tender.

6. Add the shrimp to the skillet and cook for about 3-4 minutes until they turn pink and opaque.
7. Serve the coconut-curry shrimp and vegetables over cooked brown rice.

Nutritional Facts (per serving without rice): Calories: 260 | Total Fat: 19g | Saturated Fat: 14g | Cholesterol: 170mg | Sodium: 550mg | Total Carbohydrates: 11g | Dietary Fiber: 2g | Sugars: 5g | Protein: 14g

13. Teriyaki Glazed Salmon with Steamed Asparagus

Introduction: Teriyaki Glazed Salmon with Steamed Asparagus is a sweet and savory heart-healthy dish. Salmon fillets are brushed with a flavorful teriyaki glaze and served with tender steamed asparagus.

Prep Time: 15 minutes | Cook Time: 15 minutes | Yield: 4 servings

Ingredients

For Teriyaki Glazed Salmon:

- 4 salmon fillets
- 1/4 cup low-sodium soy sauce
- 2 tablespoons honey
- 1 tablespoon rice vinegar
- 2 cloves garlic, minced
- 1 teaspoon grated fresh ginger
- Sesame seeds for garnish (optional)

For Steamed Asparagus:

- 1 bunch fresh asparagus, ends trimmed
- 1 tablespoon olive oil
- Salt and pepper to taste

Method of Preparation:

For Teriyaki Glazed Salmon:

1. In a bowl, whisk together the low-sodium soy sauce, honey, rice vinegar, minced garlic, and grated fresh ginger to create the teriyaki glaze.
2. Brush the salmon fillets generously with the teriyaki glaze.
3. Preheat the grill to medium-high heat.
4. Grill the salmon for about 4-5 minutes per side until they are cooked through and have grill marks.
5. Garnish with sesame seeds if desired.

For Steamed Asparagus:

6. While the salmon is grilling, steam the trimmed asparagus for about 3-4 minutes until they are tender but still crisp.
7. Drizzle olive oil over the steamed asparagus and season with salt and pepper.

Nutritional Facts (per serving): Calories: 320 | Total Fat: 13g | Saturated Fat: 2g | Cholesterol: 75mg | Sodium: 550mg | Total Carbohydrates: 17g | Dietary Fiber: 2g | Sugars: 13g | Protein: 34g

14. Grilled Sardines with Lemon and Fresh Herbs

Introduction: Grilled Sardines with Lemon and Fresh Herbs is a Mediterranean-inspired and heart-healthy dish. Sardines are marinated, grilled, and served with a zesty lemon and herb drizzle.

Prep Time: 15 minutes | Marinating Time: 30 minutes | Cook Time: 10 minutes | Yield: 4 servings

Ingredients

For Grilled Sardines:

- 12 fresh sardines, cleaned and gutted
- 2 tablespoons olive oil
- 2 cloves garlic, minced
- Zest and juice of 1 lemon
- Salt and pepper to taste

For Lemon and Fresh Herb Drizzle:

- 1/4 cup fresh parsley, chopped
- 1/4 cup fresh cilantro, chopped
- 1/4 cup fresh mint leaves, chopped
- 1/4 cup olive oil
- Zest and juice of 1 lemon
- Salt and pepper to taste

Method of Preparation:

For Grilled Sardines:

1. In a bowl, whisk together the olive oil, minced garlic, lemon zest, lemon juice, salt, and pepper to create the marinade.
2. Place the cleaned sardines in a shallow dish and pour the marinade over them. Cover and refrigerate for at least 30 minutes.
3. Preheat the grill to medium-high heat.
4. Grill the sardines for about 3-4 minutes per side until they are cooked through and have grill marks.

For Lemon and Fresh Herb Drizzle:

5. In a separate bowl, combine the chopped fresh parsley, chopped fresh cilantro, chopped fresh mint leaves, olive oil, lemon zest, lemon juice, salt, and pepper to create the herb drizzle.
6. Drizzle the herb mixture over the grilled sardines before serving.

Nutritional Facts (per serving): Calories: 320 | Total Fat: 24g | Saturated Fat: 4g | Cholesterol: 125mg | Sodium: 300mg | Total Carbohydrates: 4g | Dietary Fiber: 1g | Sugars: 1g | Protein: 24g

15. Baked Catfish with Avocado Salsa

Introduction: Baked Catfish with Avocado Salsa is a fresh and heart-healthy dish. Catfish fillets are seasoned, baked to perfection, and topped with a zesty avocado salsa.

Prep Time: 15 minutes | Cook Time: 20 minutes | Yield: 4 servings

Ingredients:

For Baked Catfish:

- 4 catfish fillets
- 2 tablespoons olive oil
- 1 teaspoon paprika
- 1/2 teaspoon dried thyme
- 1/2 teaspoon dried oregano
- 1/2 teaspoon garlic powder
- Salt and pepper to taste
- Lemon wedges for garnish (optional)

For Avocado Salsa:

- 2 avocados, diced
- 1 tomato, diced
- 1/4 cup red onion, finely chopped
- 1/4 cup fresh cilantro, chopped
- Juice of 1 lime
- Salt and pepper to taste

Method of Preparation:

For Baked Catfish:

1. Preheat the oven to 375°F (190°C).
2. In a small bowl, combine the olive oil, paprika, dried thyme, dried oregano, garlic

powder, salt, and pepper to create the seasoning mixture.

3. Brush both sides of the catfish fillets with the seasoning mixture.

4. Place the seasoned catfish fillets on a baking sheet lined with parchment paper.

5. Bake in the preheated oven for about 15-20 minutes or until the catfish flakes easily with a fork and is cooked through.

6. Garnish with lemon wedges if desired.

For Avocado Salsa:

7. In a bowl, combine the diced avocados, diced tomato, finely chopped red onion, chopped fresh cilantro, lime juice, salt, and pepper. Gently toss to combine.

8. Serve the baked catfish fillets with a generous scoop of avocado salsa on top.

Nutritional Facts (per serving): Calories: 300 | Total Fat: 18g | Saturated Fat: 3g | Cholesterol: 75mg | Sodium: 220mg | Total Carbohydrates: 16g | Dietary Fiber: 9g | Sugars: 2g | Protein: 25g

1. Kale and Quinoa Salad with Lemon Vinaigrette

Introduction: Kale and Quinoa Salad with Lemon Vinaigrette is a nutrient-packed and heart-healthy salad. This refreshing salad features hearty kale, protein-rich quinoa, and a zesty lemon vinaigrette.

Prep Time: 15 minutes | Cook Time: 15 minutes (for quinoa) | Yield: 4 servings

Ingredients:

For Salad:

- 4 cups kale, stems removed and chopped
- 1 cup cooked quinoa, cooled
- 1/2 cup cherry tomatoes, halved
- 1/4 cup red onion, finely chopped
- 1/4 cup grated Parmesan cheese (optional)
- 1/4 cup roasted almonds, chopped

For Lemon Vinaigrette:

- 1/4 cup extra-virgin olive oil
- Juice and zest of 1 lemon
- 2 cloves garlic, minced
- 1 teaspoon Dijon mustard
- Salt and pepper to taste

Method of Preparation:

For Salad:

1. In a large salad bowl, combine the chopped kale, cooked and cooled quinoa, halved cherry tomatoes, finely chopped red onion, grated Parmesan cheese (if using), and chopped roasted almonds.

For Lemon Vinaigrette:

2. In a separate bowl, whisk together the extra-virgin olive oil, lemon juice, lemon zest, minced garlic, Dijon mustard, salt, and pepper to create the lemon vinaigrette.

3. Drizzle the lemon vinaigrette over the salad and toss well to coat all the ingredients.
4. Let the salad sit for a few minutes to allow the flavors to meld.
5. Serve and enjoy!

Nutritional Facts (per serving): Calories: 320 | Total Fat: 22g | Saturated Fat: 3g | Cholesterol: 2mg | Sodium: 150mg | Total Carbohydrates: 26g | Dietary Fiber: 4g | Sugars: 2g | Protein: 9g

2. Mediterranean Chickpea Salad with Feta

Introduction: Mediterranean Chickpea Salad with Feta is a vibrant and heart-healthy salad inspired by Mediterranean flavors. This salad combines chickpeas, fresh vegetables, olives, and crumbled feta cheese, all tossed in a lemon-oregano dressing.

Prep Time: 15 minutes | Yield: 4 servings

Ingredients:

For Salad:

- 2 cans (15 ounces each) chickpeas, drained and rinsed
- 1 cucumber, diced
- 1 cup cherry tomatoes, halved
- 1/2 cup Kalamata olives, pitted and sliced
- 1/2 cup red onion, finely chopped
- 1/2 cup crumbled feta cheese
- 1/4 cup fresh parsley, chopped

For Lemon-Oregano Dressing:

- 1/4 cup extra-virgin olive oil
- Juice of 1 lemon
- 2 teaspoons dried oregano
- 2 cloves garlic, minced

- Salt and pepper to taste

Method of Preparation

For Salad:

1. In a large salad bowl, combine the chickpeas, diced cucumber, halved cherry tomatoes, sliced Kalamata olives, finely chopped red onion, crumbled feta cheese, and chopped fresh parsley.

For Lemon-Oregano Dressing:

2. In a separate bowl, whisk together the extra-virgin olive oil, lemon juice, dried oregano, minced garlic, salt, and pepper to create the lemon-oregano dressing.
3. Drizzle the dressing over the salad and toss well to coat all the ingredients.
4. Allow the salad to chill in the refrigerator for at least 30 minutes to let the flavors meld.
5. Serve and enjoy!

Nutritional Facts (per serving): Calories: 380 | Total Fat: 21g | Saturated Fat: 5g | Cholesterol: 17mg | Sodium: 540mg | Total Carbohydrates: 38g | Dietary Fiber: 11g | Sugars: 7g | Protein: 13g

3. Arugula and Beet Salad with Goat Cheese and Walnuts

Introduction: Arugula and Beet Salad with Goat Cheese and Walnuts is a colorful and heart-healthy salad. It features tender roasted beets, peppery arugula, creamy goat cheese, and crunchy walnuts, all drizzled with a balsamic vinaigrette.

Prep Time: 20 minutes | Cook Time: 45 minutes (for roasting beets) | Yield: 4 servings

Ingredients:

For Salad:

- 4 medium-sized beets, roasted, peeled, and sliced
- 4 cups arugula
- 1/2 cup goat cheese, crumbled
- 1/2 cup walnuts, toasted and chopped
- 1/4 cup red onion, thinly sliced

For Balsamic Vinaigrette:

- 1/4 cup extra-virgin olive oil
- 2 tablespoons balsamic vinegar
- 1 teaspoon Dijon mustard
- 1 clove garlic, minced
- Salt and pepper to taste

Method of Preparation:

For Salad:

1. Roast the beets by wrapping them in aluminum foil and placing them in a 400°F (200°C) oven for about 45 minutes, or until they are tender. Once cooled, peel and slice them.
2. In a large salad bowl, combine the arugula, sliced roasted beets, crumbled goat cheese, toasted and chopped walnuts, and thinly sliced red onion.

For Balsamic Vinaigrette:

3. In a separate bowl, whisk together the extra-virgin olive oil, balsamic vinegar, Dijon mustard, minced garlic, salt, and pepper to create the balsamic vinaigrette.
4. Drizzle the vinaigrette over the salad and toss gently to coat all the ingredients.
5. Serve and enjoy!

Nutritional Facts (per serving): Calories: 330 | Total Fat: 26g | Saturated Fat: 6g | Cholesterol: 15mg | Sodium: 280mg | Total Carbohydrates: 18g | Dietary Fiber: 5g | Sugars: 10g | Protein: 8g

4. Broccoli and Cranberry Salad with Poppy Seed Dressing

Introduction: Broccoli and Cranberry Salad with Poppy Seed Dressing is a crunchy and heart-healthy salad. This salad combines crisp broccoli florets, sweet dried cranberries, red onion, and sunflower seeds, all tossed in a creamy poppy seed dressing.

Prep Time: 20 minutes | Yield: 4 servings

Ingredients:

For Salad:

- 4 cups broccoli florets
- 1/2 cup dried cranberries
- 1/4 cup red onion, finely chopped
- 1/4 cup sunflower seeds

For Poppy Seed Dressing:

- 1/4 cup plain Greek yogurt
- 2 tablespoons mayonnaise
- 2 tablespoons honey
- 1 tablespoon apple cider vinegar
- 1 tablespoon poppy seeds
- Salt and pepper to taste

Method of Preparation:

For Salad:

1. In a large salad bowl, combine the broccoli florets, dried cranberries, finely chopped red onion, and sunflower seeds.

For Poppy Seed Dressing:

2. In a separate bowl, whisk together the plain Greek yogurt, mayonnaise, honey, apple cider vinegar, poppy seeds, salt, and pepper to create the poppy seed dressing.
3. Drizzle the dressing over the salad and toss well to coat all the ingredients.
4. Allow the salad to chill in the refrigerator for at least 30 minutes to let the flavors meld.
5. Serve and enjoy!

Nutritional Facts (per serving): Calories: 230 | Total Fat: 10g | Saturated Fat: 1g | Cholesterol: 5mg | Sodium: 130mg | Total Carbohydrates: 32g | Dietary Fiber: 5g | Sugars: 20g | Protein: 6g

5. Spinach and Strawberry Salad with Almonds

Introduction: Spinach and Strawberry Salad with Almonds is a refreshing and heart-healthy salad. This salad combines tender baby spinach leaves, sweet ripe strawberries, crunchy almonds, and a tangy balsamic vinaigrette.

Prep Time: 15 minutes | Yield: 4 servings

Ingredients:

For Salad:

- 6 cups baby spinach leaves
- 2 cups fresh strawberries, hulled and sliced
- 1/2 cup sliced almonds
- 1/4 cup red onion, thinly sliced

For Balsamic Vinaigrette:

- 1/4 cup extra-virgin olive oil
- 2 tablespoons balsamic vinegar
- 1 tablespoon honey

- 1 clove garlic, minced
- Salt and pepper to taste

Method of Preparation:

For Salad:

1. In a large salad bowl, combine the baby spinach leaves, sliced fresh strawberries, sliced almonds, and thinly sliced red onion.

For Balsamic Vinaigrette:

2. In a separate bowl, whisk together the extra-virgin olive oil, balsamic vinegar, honey, minced garlic, salt, and pepper to create the balsamic vinaigrette.
3. Drizzle the vinaigrette over the salad and toss gently to coat all the ingredients.
4. Serve and enjoy!

Nutritional Facts (per serving): Calories: 240 | Total Fat: 18g | Saturated Fat: 2g | Cholesterol: 0mg | Sodium: 85mg | Total Carbohydrates: 19g | Dietary Fiber: 4g | Sugars: 12g | Protein: 5g

6. Avocado and Tomato Salad with Basil and Balsamic

Introduction: Avocado and Tomato Salad with Basil and Balsamic is a simple and heart-healthy salad. This salad showcases ripe avocados and juicy tomatoes, drizzled with a flavorful balsamic glaze and garnished with fresh basil.

Prep Time: 10 minutes | Yield: 4 servings

Ingredients:

For Salad:

- 2 ripe avocados, diced
- 2 large tomatoes, diced

- 1/4 cup fresh basil leaves, torn
- 1/4 cup red onion, finely chopped

For Balsamic Glaze:

- 1/4 cup balsamic vinegar
- 1 tablespoon honey
- Salt and pepper to taste

Method of Preparation:

For Salad:

1. In a salad bowl, combine the diced ripe avocados, diced tomatoes, torn fresh basil leaves, and finely chopped red onion.

For Balsamic Glaze:

2. In a small saucepan, whisk together the balsamic vinegar, honey, salt, and pepper. Bring to a simmer over low heat and cook for a few minutes until the glaze thickens slightly.
3. Remove from heat and let it cool.
4. Drizzle the balsamic glaze over the salad just before serving.

Nutritional Facts (per serving): Calories: 190 | Total Fat: 14g | Saturated Fat: 2g | Cholesterol: 0mg | Sodium: 10mg | Total Carbohydrates: 17g | Dietary Fiber: 6g | Sugars: 8g | Protein: 2g

7. Tuna Salad with Avocado Mayo

Introduction: Tuna Salad with Avocado Mayo is a creamy and heart-healthy twist on traditional tuna salad. It features canned tuna mixed with a rich and creamy avocado-based mayo, making it a flavorful and nutritious option.

Prep Time: 10 minutes | Yield: 4 servings

Ingredients:

For Tuna Salad:

- 2 cans (5 ounces each) canned tuna, drained
- 1/2 cup celery, finely chopped
- 1/4 cup red onion, finely chopped
- 1/4 cup dill pickles, finely chopped

For Avocado Mayo:

- 2 ripe avocados, peeled and pitted
- 1 tablespoon lemon juice
- 1 clove garlic, minced
- Salt and pepper to taste

Method of Preparation:

For Tuna Salad:

1. In a mixing bowl, combine the drained canned tuna, finely chopped celery, finely chopped red onion, and finely chopped dill pickles.

For Avocado Mayo:

2. In a separate bowl, mash the ripe avocados with a fork until smooth.
3. Add lemon juice, minced garlic, salt, and pepper to the mashed avocados, creating the avocado mayo.
4. Fold the avocado mayo into the tuna salad mixture until well combined.
5. Chill the tuna salad in the refrigerator for about 30 minutes before serving.

Nutritional Facts (per serving): Calories: 220 | Total Fat: 11g | Saturated Fat: 1.5g | Cholesterol: 20mg | Sodium: 340mg | Total Carbohydrates: 12g | Dietary Fiber: 6g | Sugars: 2g | Protein: 19g

8. Greek Salad with Feta and Kalamata Olives

Introduction: Greek Salad with Feta and Kalamata Olives is a classic Mediterranean-inspired salad. It combines crisp cucumbers, juicy tomatoes, red onions, creamy feta cheese, and briny Kalamata olives, all tossed in a Greek vinaigrette.

Prep Time: 15 minutes | Yield: 4 servings

Ingredients:

For Salad:

- 2 large cucumbers, diced
- 2 large tomatoes, diced
- 1/2 cup red onion, thinly sliced
- 1/2 cup Kalamata olives, pitted and sliced
- 1/2 cup crumbled feta cheese
- 1/4 cup fresh parsley, chopped

For Greek Vinaigrette:

- 1/4 cup extra-virgin olive oil
- 2 tablespoons red wine vinegar
- 1 teaspoon dried oregano
- 1 clove garlic, minced
- Salt and pepper to taste

Method of Preparation:

For Salad:

1. In a large salad bowl, combine the diced cucumbers, diced tomatoes, thinly sliced red onion, sliced Kalamata olives, crumbled feta cheese, and chopped fresh parsley.

For Greek Vinaigrette:

2. In a separate bowl, whisk together the extra-virgin olive oil, red wine vinegar, dried oregano, minced garlic, salt, and pepper to create the Greek vinaigrette.

3. Drizzle the vinaigrette over the salad and toss gently to coat all the ingredients.
4. Allow the salad to chill in the refrigerator for at least 30 minutes to let the flavors meld.
5. Serve and enjoy!

Nutritional Facts (per serving): Calories: 280 | Total Fat: 22g | Saturated Fat: 6g | Cholesterol: 25mg | Sodium: 550mg | Total Carbohydrates: 15g | Dietary Fiber: 4g | Sugars: 7g | Protein: 7g

9. Roasted Vegetable Salad with Balsamic Reduction

Introduction: Roasted Vegetable Salad with Balsamic Reduction is a flavorful and heart-healthy salad. It features an assortment of roasted vegetables drizzled with a sweet balsamic reduction for a delightful mix of textures and flavors.

Prep Time: 20 minutes | Cook Time: 30 minutes (for roasting vegetables) | Yield: 4 servings

Ingredients:

For Salad:

- 4 cups mixed roasted vegetables (bell peppers, zucchini, cherry tomatoes, etc.)
- 1/4 cup red onion, thinly sliced
- 1/4 cup crumbled goat cheese
- 1/4 cup fresh basil leaves, torn
- 1/4 cup toasted pine nuts

For Balsamic Reduction:

- 1/2 cup balsamic vinegar
- 2 tablespoons honey
- Salt and pepper to taste

Method of Preparation:

For Salad:

1. Preheat the oven to 400°F (200°C).
2. Toss the mixed vegetables with a drizzle of olive oil, salt, and pepper, then spread them on a baking sheet.
3. Roast in the preheated oven for about 30 minutes or until the vegetables are tender and slightly caramelized. Let them cool.
4. In a large salad bowl, combine the roasted vegetables, thinly sliced red onion, crumbled goat cheese, torn fresh basil leaves, and toasted pine nuts.

For Balsamic Reduction:

- In a small saucepan, combine the balsamic vinegar and honey. Simmer over low heat until the mixture reduces by half and thickens.
- Remove from heat and let it cool.
- Drizzle the balsamic reduction over the salad just before serving.

Nutritional Facts (per serving): Calories: 250 | Total Fat: 11g | Saturated Fat: 2g | Cholesterol: 5mg | Sodium: 45mg | Total Carbohydrates: 35g | Dietary Fiber: 5g | Sugars: 22g | Protein: 6g

10. Three-Bean Salad with Dijon Dressing

Introduction: Three-Bean Salad with Dijon Dressing is a hearty and heart-healthy salad. It combines three types of beans—green beans, kidney beans, and cannellini beans—with a tangy Dijon mustard dressing for a flavorful and protein-rich dish.

Prep Time: 15 minutes | Cook Time: 5 minutes (for blanching green beans) | Yield: 4 servings

Ingredients:

For Salad:

- 1 cup green beans, trimmed and blanched
- 1 can (15 ounces) kidney beans, drained and rinsed
- 1 can (15 ounces) cannellini beans, drained and rinsed
- 1/4 cup red onion, finely chopped
- 1/4 cup fresh parsley, chopped

For Dijon Dressing:

- 2 tablespoons extra-virgin olive oil
- 2 tablespoons red wine vinegar
- 1 tablespoon Dijon mustard
- 1 clove garlic, minced
- Salt and pepper to taste

Method of Preparation:

For Salad:

1. Blanch the green beans in boiling water for about 2-3 minutes until they are bright green, then immediately transfer them to ice water to cool. Drain and chop into bite-sized pieces.
2. In a large salad bowl, combine the blanched green beans, kidney beans, cannellini beans, finely chopped red onion, and chopped fresh parsley.

For Dijon Dressing:

3. In a separate bowl, whisk together the extra-virgin olive oil, red wine vinegar, Dijon mustard, minced garlic, salt, and pepper to create the Dijon dressing.
4. Drizzle the dressing over the salad and toss gently to coat all the ingredients.
5. Let the salad chill in the refrigerator for at least 30 minutes to allow the flavors to meld.
6. Serve and enjoy!

Nutritional Facts (per serving): Calories: 280 | Total Fat: 8g | Saturated Fat: 1g | Cholesterol: 0mg | Sodium: 380mg | Total Carbohydrates: 43g | Dietary Fiber: 13g | Sugars: 6g | Protein: 12g

11. Cucumber and Red Onion Salad with Dill

Introduction: Cucumber and Red Onion Salad with Dill is a crisp and heart-healthy salad. It combines thinly sliced cucumbers, red onions, and fresh dill in a light vinegar-based dressing for a refreshing and tangy side dish.

Prep Time: 15 minutes | Yield: 4 servings

Ingredients:

For Salad:

- 2 large cucumbers, thinly sliced
- 1/2 red onion, thinly sliced
- 2 tablespoons fresh dill, chopped

For Dressing:

- 1/4 cup white vinegar
- 2 tablespoons extra-virgin olive oil
- 1 tablespoon sugar (or a sugar substitute)
- Salt and pepper to taste

Method of Preparation:

For Salad:

1. In a large salad bowl, combine the thinly sliced cucumbers, thinly sliced red onion, and chopped fresh dill.

For Dressing:

2. In a small bowl, whisk together the white vinegar, extra-virgin olive oil, sugar (or sugar substitute), salt, and pepper to create the dressing.

3. Drizzle the dressing over the salad and toss gently to coat all the ingredients.

4. Allow the salad to chill in the refrigerator for at least 15 minutes to let the flavors meld.

5. Serve and enjoy!

Nutritional Facts (per serving): Calories: 80 | Total Fat: 5g | Saturated Fat: 0.5g | Cholesterol: 0mg | Sodium: 5mg | Total Carbohydrates: 9g | Dietary Fiber: 1g | Sugars: 5g | Protein: 1g

12. Asparagus and Cherry Tomato Salad with Lemon

Introduction: Asparagus and Cherry Tomato Salad with Lemon is a vibrant and heart-healthy salad that celebrates the flavors of fresh asparagus and juicy cherry tomatoes. It's enhanced with a zesty lemon dressing for a burst of citrusy freshness.

Prep Time: 15 minutes | Cook Time: 5 minutes (for blanching asparagus) | Yield: 4 servings

Ingredients:

For Salad:

- 1 bunch asparagus, trimmed and blanched
- 2 cups cherry tomatoes, halved
- 1/4 cup red onion, finely chopped
- 2 tablespoons fresh basil leaves, torn

For Lemon Dressing:

- Juice and zest of 1 lemon
- 2 tablespoons extra-virgin olive oil
- 1 clove garlic, minced
- Salt and pepper to taste

Method of Preparation:

For Salad:

1. Blanch the asparagus in boiling water for about 2-3 minutes until they are bright green, then immediately transfer them to ice water to cool. Drain and cut into bite-sized pieces.
2. In a large salad bowl, combine the blanched asparagus, halved cherry tomatoes, finely chopped red onion, and torn fresh basil leaves.

For Lemon Dressing:

3. In a small bowl, whisk together the lemon juice, lemon zest, extra-virgin olive oil, minced garlic, salt, and pepper to create the lemon dressing.
4. Drizzle the dressing over the salad and toss gently to coat all the ingredients.
5. Let the salad chill in the refrigerator for at least 15 minutes to allow the flavors to meld.
6. Serve and enjoy!

Nutritional Facts (per serving): Calories: 90 | Total Fat: 7g | Saturated Fat: 1g | Cholesterol: 0mg | Sodium: 10mg | Total Carbohydrates: 7g | Dietary Fiber: 2g | Sugars: 3g| Protein: 2g

13. Waldorf Salad with Greek Yogurt Dressing

Introduction: Waldorf Salad with Greek Yogurt Dressing is a creamy and heart-healthy twist on the classic Waldorf salad. It features crisp apples, crunchy celery, sweet grapes, and walnuts, all coated in a creamy Greek yogurt-based dressing.

Prep Time: 15 minutes | Yield: 4 servings

Ingredients:

For Salad:

- 2 apples, diced
- 1 cup celery, thinly sliced
- 1 cup red grapes, halved
- 1/2 cup walnuts, chopped
- 1/4 cup raisins (optional)

For Greek Yogurt Dressing:

- 1/2 cup plain Greek yogurt
- 2 tablespoons honey
- 1 tablespoon lemon juice
- 1/4 teaspoon ground cinnamon
- Salt to taste

Method of Preparation:

For Salad:

1. In a large salad bowl, combine the diced apples, thinly sliced celery, halved red grapes, chopped walnuts, and optional raisins.

For Greek Yogurt Dressing:

2. In a separate bowl, whisk together the plain Greek yogurt, honey, lemon juice, ground cinnamon, and a pinch of salt to create the Greek yogurt dressing.
3. Drizzle the dressing over the salad and toss gently to coat all the ingredients.
4. Serve and enjoy!

Nutritional Facts (per serving): Calories: 260 | Total Fat: 11g | Saturated Fat: 1.5g | Cholesterol: 0mg | Sodium: 35mg | Total Carbohydrates: 40g | Dietary Fiber: 6g | Sugars: 29g | Protein: 7g

14. Spinach and Orange Salad with Candied Walnuts

Introduction: Spinach and Orange Salad with Candied Walnuts is a vibrant and heart-healthy salad. It combines fresh baby spinach leaves, juicy orange segments, and candied walnuts, all drizzled with a zesty orange vinaigrette.

Prep Time: 15 minutes | Yield: 4 servings

Ingredients:

For Salad:

- 6 cups baby spinach leaves
- 2 large oranges, peeled and segmented
- 1/2 cup candied walnuts
- 1/4 cup red onion, thinly sliced
- 1/4 cup crumbled goat cheese (optional)

For Orange Vinaigrette:

- Juice and zest of 1 orange
- 2 tablespoons extra-virgin olive oil
- 1 tablespoon honey
- 1/4 teaspoon Dijon mustard
- Salt and pepper to taste

Method of Preparation:

For Salad:

1. In a large salad bowl, combine the baby spinach leaves, orange segments, candied walnuts, thinly sliced red onion, and crumbled goat cheese (if desired).

For Orange Vinaigrette:

2. In a small bowl, whisk together the orange juice, orange zest, extra-virgin olive oil, honey, Dijon mustard, salt, and pepper to create the orange vinaigrette.
3. Drizzle the vinaigrette over the salad and toss gently to coat all the ingredients.

4. Serve and enjoy!

Nutritional Facts (per serving): Calories: 260 | Total Fat: 16g | Saturated Fat: 2.5g | Cholesterol: 5mg | Sodium: 140mg | Total Carbohydrates: 29g | Dietary Fiber: 5g | Sugars: 20g | Protein: 5g

15. Quinoa and Avocado Salad with Lime Dressing

Introduction: Quinoa and Avocado Salad with Lime Dressing is a nutritious and heart-healthy salad. It features fluffy quinoa, creamy avocado, black beans, and corn, all tossed in a zesty lime dressing for a satisfying and flavorful dish.

Prep Time: 20 minutes | Cook Time: 15 minutes (for cooking quinoa) | Yield: 4 servings

Ingredients:

For Salad:

- 1 cup quinoa, rinsed and cooked
- 2 ripe avocados, diced
- 1 can (15 ounces) black beans, drained and rinsed
- 1 cup corn kernels (fresh or frozen)
- 1/4 cup red onion, finely chopped
- 1/4 cup fresh cilantro, chopped

For Lime Dressing:

- Juice and zest of 2 limes
- 2 tablespoons extra-virgin olive oil
- 1 clove garlic, minced
- 1/2 teaspoon ground cumin
- Salt and pepper to taste

Method of Preparation

For Salad:

1. Cook the quinoa according to package instructions and let it cool to room temperature.
2. In a large salad bowl, combine the cooked quinoa, diced ripe avocados, black beans, corn kernels, finely chopped red onion, and chopped fresh cilantro.

For Lime Dressing:

3. In a small bowl, whisk together the lime juice, lime zest, extra-virgin olive oil, minced garlic, ground cumin, salt, and pepper to create the lime dressing.
4. Drizzle the dressing over the salad and toss gently to coat all the ingredients.
5. Let the salad chill in the refrigerator for at least 15 minutes to allow the flavors to meld.
6. Serve and enjoy!

Nutritional Facts (per serving): Calories: 410 | Total Fat: 20g | Saturated Fat: 3g | Cholesterol: 0mg | Sodium: 120mg | Total Carbohydrates: 50g | Dietary Fiber: 15g | Sugars: 2g | Protein: 12g

1. Dark Chocolate-Dipped Strawberries:

Introduction: These luscious dark chocolate-dipped strawberries are a delightful treat that satisfies your sweet tooth while providing heart-healthy antioxidants from dark chocolate.

Prep Time: 15 minutes | Cook Time: 5 minutes (for melting chocolate) | Yield: Approximately 24 dipped strawberries

Ingredients

- 24 fresh strawberries, washed and dried
- 8 ounces (about 1 1/2 cups) dark chocolate chips (70% cocoa or higher)

Method of Preparation:

1. Line a baking sheet with parchment paper.
2. In a microwave-safe bowl, melt the dark chocolate chips in 30-second intervals, stirring until smooth.
3. Hold each strawberry by the green stem and dip it into the melted chocolate, coating about two-thirds of the strawberry.
4. Place the dipped strawberries on the prepared baking sheet.
5. Allow the chocolate to set at room temperature or in the refrigerator until firm.

Nutritional Facts (per dipped strawberry): | Calories: 45 | Total Fat: 2.5g | Cholesterol: 0mg | Sodium: 0mg | Total Carbohydrates: 6g | Dietary Fiber: 1g | Sugars: 4g | Protein: 1g

2. Baked Apples with Cinnamon and Walnuts

Introduction: Enjoy the comforting flavors of baked apples with a touch of cinnamon and the crunch of heart-healthy walnuts in this wholesome dessert or snack option.

Prep Time: 10 minutes | Cook Time: 30 minutes | Yield: 4 servings

Ingredients:

- 4 apples (such as Granny Smith or Honeycrisp), cored and halved
- 2 tablespoons chopped walnuts
- 2 tablespoons honey
- 1 teaspoon ground cinnamon
- 1/4 cup water

Method of Preparation:

1. Preheat the oven to 350°F (175°C).
2. Place the apple halves, cut side up, in a baking dish.
3. In a small bowl, mix the chopped walnuts, honey, and ground cinnamon.
4. Spoon the walnut mixture evenly into the apple halves.
5. Pour the water into the bottom of the baking dish.
6. Cover the dish with foil and bake for 20-25 minutes, or until the apples are tender.
7. Remove the foil and bake for an additional 5-10 minutes to allow the tops to brown slightly.

Nutritional Facts (per serving): Calories: 170 | Total Fat: 2.5g | Cholesterol: 0mg | Sodium: 0mg | Total Carbohydrates: 39g | Dietary Fiber: 6g | Sugars: 29g | Protein: 1g

3. Frozen Banana Bites with Almond Butter and Dark Chocolate

Introduction: These frozen banana bites combine the creaminess of ripe bananas, the richness of almond butter, and the decadence of dark chocolate, creating a satisfying and nutritious treat.

Prep Time: 15 minutes | Cook Time: 0 minutes (freezing time required) | Yield: Approximately 24 banana bites

Ingredients:

- 2 large ripe bananas
- 1/4 cup almond butter
- 4 ounces (about 3/4 cup) dark chocolate chips (70% cocoa or higher)
- 1 tablespoon coconut oil (for melting chocolate)

Method of Preparation:

1. Line a baking sheet with parchment paper.
2. Slice the bananas into 1/2-inch-thick rounds.
3. Spread almond butter onto half of the banana rounds and top with the remaining rounds to create banana "sandwiches."
4. In a microwave-safe bowl, melt the dark chocolate chips and coconut oil in 30-second intervals, stirring until smooth.
5. Dip each banana "sandwich" into the melted chocolate, allowing excess chocolate to drip off.
6. Place the dipped banana bites on the prepared baking sheet.
7. Freeze for at least 2 hours or until firm.

Nutritional Facts (per banana bite): Calories: 60 | Total Fat: 4g | Cholesterol: 0mg | Sodium:

0mg | Total Carbohydrates: 7g | Dietary Fiber: 1g | Sugars: 4g | Protein: 1g

| Total Carbohydrates: 23g | Dietary Fiber: 10g | Sugars: 9g | Protein: 5g

4. Chia Seed Pudding with Dark Chocolate and Raspberries

Introduction: Indulge in a guilt-free dessert with this chia seed pudding infused with the bold flavors of dark chocolate and the tart sweetness of fresh raspberries.

Prep Time: 5 minutes (plus chilling time) | Cook Time: 0 minutes Yield: 4 servings

Ingredients:

- 1/2 cup chia seeds
- 2 cups unsweetened almond milk
- 2 tablespoons unsweetened cocoa powder
- 2 tablespoons honey or maple syrup
- 1/2 cup fresh raspberries
- 2 tablespoons dark chocolate chips (70% cocoa or higher)

Method of Preparation:

1. In a mixing bowl, combine the chia seeds, almond milk, cocoa powder, and honey (or maple syrup). Stir well.
2. Cover the bowl and refrigerate for at least 4 hours or overnight, allowing the mixture to thicken.
3. Before serving, stir the pudding to ensure a smooth consistency.
4. Divide the chia seed pudding into serving glasses.
5. Top each serving with fresh raspberries and a sprinkle of dark chocolate chips.

Nutritional Facts (per serving): Calories: 180 | Total Fat: 9g | Cholesterol: 0mg | Sodium: 0mg

5. Greek Yogurt and Mixed Berry Parfait

Introduction: This Greek yogurt and mixed berry parfait is a delightful blend of creamy yogurt, vibrant berries, and a drizzle of honey, making it a perfect choice for a healthy dessert or breakfast.

Prep Time: 10 minutes | Cook Time: 0 minutes | Yield: 2 servings

Ingredients:

- 1 cup Greek yogurt
- 2 tablespoons honey
- 1/4 cup granola (optional for added crunch)

Method of Preparation:

1. In two serving glasses or bowls, begin by layering a spoonful of Greek yogurt at the bottom.
2. Add a layer of mixed berries on top of the yogurt.
3. Drizzle a bit of honey over the berries.
4. Repeat the layers until the glass is filled.
5. If desired, sprinkle granola on the top layer for added texture.

Nutritional Facts (per serving, without granola): Calories: 200 | Total Fat: 2g | Cholesterol: 10mg | Sodium: 50mg | Total Carbohydrates: 36g | Dietary Fiber: 3g | Sugars: 29g | Protein: 12g

6. Almond and Date Energy Bites

Introduction: These almond and date energy bites are packed with heart-healthy almonds and naturally sweet dates, providing a quick and nutritious energy boost.

Prep Time: 15 minutes | Cook Time: 0 minutes | Yield: Approximately 12 energy bites

Ingredients:

- 1 cup almonds
- 1 cup pitted dates
- 2 tablespoons unsweetened cocoa powder
- 1 teaspoon vanilla extract
- A pinch of salt

Method of Preparation:

1. Place almonds in a food processor and pulse until finely chopped.
2. Add pitted dates, cocoa powder, vanilla extract, and a pinch of salt to the food processor. Blend until the mixture starts to come together.
3. Roll the mixture into bite-sized balls and place them on a parchment-lined tray.
4. Refrigerate for about 30 minutes to firm up.

Nutritional Facts (per energy bite): Calories: 90 | Total Fat: 4g | Cholesterol: 0mg | Sodium: 0mg | Total Carbohydrates: 13g | Dietary Fiber: 2g | Sugars: 9g | Protein: 2g

7. Oatmeal Raisin Cookies with Oat Flour and Raisins:

Introduction: Enjoy the classic taste of oatmeal raisin cookies made with wholesome oat flour and plump raisins, creating a delicious and heart-friendly treat.

Prep Time: 15 minutes | Cook Time: 10 minutes | Yield: Approximately 20 cookies

Ingredients:

- 2 cups oat flour (made by blending rolled oats)
- 1 teaspoon baking powder
- 1/2 teaspoon baking soda
- 1/2 teaspoon ground cinnamon
- 1/4 teaspoon salt
- 1/2 cup unsalted butter, softened
- 1/2 cup honey or maple syrup
- 1 large egg
- 1 teaspoon vanilla extract
- 1 cup raisins

Method of Preparation:

1. Preheat the oven to 350°F (175°C) and line a baking sheet with parchment paper.
2. In a mixing bowl, combine oat flour, baking powder, baking soda, cinnamon, and salt.
3. In a separate bowl, cream together the softened butter and honey (or maple syrup) until well combined.
4. Beat in the egg and vanilla extract.
5. Gradually add the dry ingredients to the wet ingredients and mix until a dough forms.
6. Stir in the raisins.
7. Drop spoonfuls of dough onto the prepared baking sheet and flatten each cookie slightly.
8. Bake for 8-10 minutes, or until the edges are golden brown.
9. Allow the cookies to cool on a wire rack.

Nutritional Facts (per cookie): Calories: 100 | Total Fat: 4g | Cholesterol: 20mg | Sodium: 75mg | Total Carbohydrates: 16g | Dietary Fiber: 1g | Sugars: 8g | Protein: 1g

8. Avocado Chocolate Mousse with Cocoa Powder

Introduction: Indulge in the velvety goodness of this avocado chocolate mousse, a dessert that uses avocado for creaminess and cocoa powder for a bold chocolate flavor.

Prep Time: 10 minutes | Cook Time: 0 minutes | Yield: 4 servings

Ingredients:

- 2 ripe avocados, peeled and pitted
- 1/2 cup unsweetened cocoa powder
- 1/4 cup honey or maple syrup
- 1 teaspoon vanilla extract
- A pinch of salt
- 1/4 cup unsweetened almond milk (or milk of choice)

Method of Preparation

1. Place the avocados, cocoa powder, honey (or maple syrup), vanilla extract, salt, and almond milk in a blender or food processor.
2. Blend until the mixture is smooth and creamy, scraping down the sides as needed.
3. Divide the mousse into serving cups or glasses.
4. Refrigerate for at least 30 minutes before serving.

Nutritional Facts (per serving): Calories: 230 | Total Fat: 13g | Cholesterol: 0mg | Sodium: 10mg | Total Carbohydrates: 34g | Dietary Fiber: 9g | Sugars: 20g | Protein: 3g

9. Mixed Berry Sorbet with Fresh Berries

Introduction: This mixed berry sorbet is a refreshing and cholesterol-friendly dessert made with a medley of fresh, vibrant berries.

Prep Time: 10 minutes (plus freezing time) | Cook Time: 0 minutes | Yield: Approximately 4 servings

Ingredients:

- 2 cups mixed berries (such as strawberries, blueberries, and raspberries), frozen
- 1/4 cup honey or maple syrup
- 1 tablespoon lemon juice
- Fresh berries for garnish (optional)

Method of Preparation:

1. In a blender or food processor, combine the frozen mixed berries, honey (or maple syrup), and lemon juice.
2. Blend until the mixture is smooth and creamy.
3. If needed, adjust sweetness with more honey or maple syrup.
4. Transfer the sorbet mixture to an airtight container and freeze for at least 2-3 hours to firm up.
5. Serve the sorbet in bowls or glasses, garnished with fresh berries if desired.

Nutritional Facts (per serving): Calories: 100 | Total Fat: 0.5g | Cholesterol: 0mg | Sodium: 0mg | Total Carbohydrates: 26g | Dietary Fiber: 3g | Sugars: 21g | Protein: 1g

10. Poached Pears in Red Wine with Cinnamon

Introduction: Poached pears in red wine with a hint of cinnamon offer a sophisticated dessert option that's not only flavorful but also heart-conscious.

Prep Time: 10 minutes | Cook Time: 30 minutes | Yield: 4 servings

Ingredients:

- 4 ripe pears, peeled and cored
- 1 bottle (750ml) red wine (such as Cabernet Sauvignon)
- 1 cup granulated sugar
- 2 cinnamon sticks
- Zest of 1 orange (optional)

Method of Preparation:

1. In a large saucepan, combine the red wine, granulated sugar, cinnamon sticks, and orange zest (if using).
2. Heat the mixture over medium heat, stirring until the sugar dissolves.
3. Reduce the heat to low and add the peeled and cored pears to the wine mixture.
4. Simmer for about 25-30 minutes, or until the pears are tender but not mushy, turning them occasionally.
5. Remove the pears from the poaching liquid and allow them to cool slightly.
6. Continue to simmer the poaching liquid until it reduces and thickens into a syrup, about 10-15 minutes.
7. Serve each pear drizzled with the red wine syrup.

Nutritional Facts (per serving): Calories: 300 | Total Fat: 0g | Cholesterol: 0mg || Sodium: 0mg| Total Carbohydrates: 64g | Dietary Fiber: 6g | Sugars: 45g | Protein: 1g

11. Pumpkin and Walnut Oat Bars with Spices

Introduction: These pumpkin and walnut oat bars are a harmonious blend of seasonal spices, heart-healthy walnuts, and the natural sweetness of pumpkin.

Prep Time: 15 minutes | Cook Time: 25 minutes | Yield: Approximately 12 bars

Ingredients:

- 2 cups old-fashioned oats
- 1 cup pumpkin puree (canned or homemade)
- 1/2 cup chopped walnuts
- 1/2 cup honey or maple syrup
- 1 teaspoon ground cinnamon
- 1/2 teaspoon ground nutmeg
- 1/2 teaspoon ground ginger
- 1/4 teaspoon ground cloves
- 1/4 teaspoon salt

Method of Preparation:

1. Preheat the oven to 350°F (175°C) and grease or line an 8x8-inch baking pan.
2. In a large mixing bowl, combine oats, chopped walnuts, cinnamon, nutmeg, ginger, cloves, and salt.
3. In a separate bowl, mix together the pumpkin puree and honey (or maple syrup) until well combined.
4. Add the wet mixture to the dry ingredients and stir until everything is evenly incorporated.
5. Press the mixture into the prepared baking pan.
6. Bake for 25-30 minutes, or until the edges are golden brown.

7. Allow the bars to cool in the pan before cutting them into squares.

Nutritional Facts (per bar): Calories: 160 | Total Fat: 5g | Cholesterol: 0mg | Sodium: 40mg | Total Carbohydrates: 27g | Dietary Fiber: 3g | Sugars: 14g | Protein: 3g

12. Coconut and Lime Rice Pudding with Unsweetened Coconut

Introduction: Delight in the tropical flavors of coconut and lime in this creamy rice pudding made with unsweetened coconut for a heart-conscious dessert.

Prep Time: 10 minutes | Cook Time: 30 minutes | Yield: Approximately 6 servings

Ingredients:

- 1 cup Arborio rice
- 4 cups unsweetened coconut milk
- 1/2 cup granulated sugar or sweetener of choice
- Zest and juice of 2 limes
- 1/2 cup unsweetened shredded coconut

Method of Preparation:

1. Rinse the Arborio rice under cold water and drain.
2. In a large saucepan, combine the rinsed rice, unsweetened coconut milk, and granulated sugar.
3. Bring the mixture to a simmer over medium heat, stirring frequently.
4. Reduce the heat to low and simmer, stirring occasionally, for about 25-30 minutes, or until the rice is tender and the mixture thickens.
5. Stir in the lime zest and lime juice.
6. Remove the rice pudding from heat and let it cool slightly.
7. Toast the unsweetened shredded coconut in a dry skillet over medium heat until lightly browned.
8. Serve the rice pudding warm or chilled, garnished with toasted coconut.

Nutritional Facts (per serving): Calories: 250 | Total Fat: 7g | Cholesterol: 0mg | Sodium: 15mg | Total Carbohydrates: 45g | Dietary Fiber: 2g | Sugars: 19g | | Protein: 2g

13. Chocolate Avocado Truffles with Cocoa Powder

Introduction: Savor the richness of chocolate avocado truffles, a decadent treat that uses avocado to create a creamy texture and cocoa powder for a bold chocolate taste.

Prep Time: 20 minutes (plus chilling time) | Cook Time: 0 minutes | Yield: Approximately 20 truffles

Ingredients:

- 2 ripe avocados, peeled and pitted
- 1/2 cup unsweetened cocoa powder
- 1/4 cup honey or maple syrup
- 1 teaspoon vanilla extract
- A pinch of salt
- Unsweetened cocoa powder for rolling

Method of Preparation:

1. In a food processor or blender, combine the ripe avocados, unsweetened cocoa powder,

honey (or maple syrup), vanilla extract, and a pinch of salt.
2. Blend until the mixture is smooth and creamy.
3. Transfer the mixture to a bowl and refrigerate for about 30 minutes to firm up.
4. Once chilled, scoop out small portions of the mixture and roll them into truffle-sized balls.
5. Roll each truffle in unsweetened cocoa powder to coat.
6. Place the truffles on a parchment-lined tray and refrigerate until ready to serve.

Nutritional Facts (per truffle): Calories: 50 | Total Fat: 3.5g | Cholesterol: 0mg | Sodium: 0mg | Total Carbohydrates: 6g | Dietary Fiber: 2g | Sugars: 3g | Protein: 1g

Method of Preparation:

1. In a blender, combine the frozen mango chunks, Greek yogurt, unsweetened shredded coconut, and honey (or maple syrup).
2. Blend until the mixture is smooth and creamy.
3. Transfer the frozen yogurt mixture to an airtight container and freeze for at least 2-3 hours until firm.
4. Serve the frozen yogurt in bowls, garnished with toasted coconut flakes if desired.

Nutritional Facts (per serving): Calories: 190 | Total Fat: 5g | Cholesterol: 5mg | Sodium: 20mg | Total Carbohydrates: 32g | Dietary Fiber: 3g | Sugars: 26g | Protein: 7g

14. Mango and Coconut Frozen Yogurt with Toasted Coconut Flakes

Introduction: This mango and coconut frozen yogurt combines the tropical flavors of mango and coconut with the crunch of toasted coconut flakes for a delightful and healthy dessert.

Prep Time: 10 minutes (plus freezing time) | Cook Time: 0 minutes | Yield: Approximately 4 servings

Ingredients:

- 2 cups frozen mango chunks
- 1 cup Greek yogurt (full-fat or low-fat)
- 1/4 cup unsweetened shredded coconut
- 2 tablespoons honey or maple syrup
- Toasted coconut flakes for garnish (optional)

15. Pistachio and Berry Crumble with Oat Topping

Introduction: Enjoy the nutty goodness of pistachios and the sweetness of berries in this irresistible crumble topped with heart-healthy oats.

Prep Time: 15 minutes | Cook Time: 30 minutes | Yield: Approximately 6 servings

Ingredients:

- 2 cups mixed berries (such as blueberries, strawberries, and raspberries)
- 1/2 cup shelled pistachios, chopped
- 1/4 cup granulated sugar or sweetener of choice
- 1 tablespoon lemon juice
- 1/2 cup old-fashioned oats
- 1/4 cup whole wheat flour
- 1/4 cup unsalted butter, cold and diced

- A pinch of salt

Method of Preparation:

1. Preheat the oven to 350°F (175°C).
2. In a mixing bowl, combine the mixed berries, chopped pistachios, granulated sugar, and lemon juice. Toss to coat the berries.
3. In a separate bowl, combine the oats, whole wheat flour, cold diced butter, and a pinch of salt. Use your fingers or a pastry cutter to blend the mixture until it resembles coarse crumbs.
4. Spread the berry mixture evenly in a baking dish.
5. Sprinkle the oat topping over the berries.
6. Bake for 25-30 minutes, or until the topping is golden brown and the berries are bubbling.
7. Allow the crumble to cool slightly before serving.

Nutritional Facts (per serving): Calories: 280 | Total Fat: 15g | Cholesterol: 20mg | Sodium: 10mg | Total Carbohydrates: 35g | Dietary Fiber: 6g | Sugars: 15g | Protein: 5g

RECIPES INDEX

Edamame with Sea Salt	29
Frozen Banana Bites with Almond Butter and Dark Chocolate	78
Garlic Butter Shrimp and Broccoli	56
Golden Turmeric Latte	24
Greek Salad with Feta and Kalamata Olives	71
Greek Yogurt and Mixed Berry Parfait	79
Greek Yogurt Parfait with Mixed Berries	11
Greek Yogurt with Honey and Walnuts	30
Green Smoothie with Kale and Mango	17
Green Tea and Lemon Detox Drink	20
Grilled Chicken Breast with Lemon and Herbs	45
Grilled Portobello Mushrooms with Balsamic Glaze	52
Grilled Sardines with Lemon and Fresh Herbs	63
Grilled Tuna Steak with Mango Salsa	55
Ground Chicken Lettuce Wraps with Asian Sauce	50
Herb-Crusted Mahi-Mahi with Quinoa	61
Kale and Pineapple Smoothie with Chia Seeds	21
Kale and Quinoa Salad with Lemon Vinaigrette	66
Lean Beef and Broccoli Stir-Fry	47
Lemon Garlic Shrimp Skewers	48
Lemon Garlic Tilapia Fillets	58
Lemon Herb Couscous with Chickpeas and Olives	44
Lentil and Vegetable Curry	35
Mango and Coconut Frozen Yogurt with Toasted Coconut Flakes	84
Mediterranean Chickpea Salad with Feta	67
Miso Glazed Salmon with Bok Choy	57
Mixed Berry Sorbet with Fresh Berries	81
Mixed Nuts and Dried Cranberries	29
Oatmeal Raisin Cookies with Oat Flour and Raisins:	80
Oatmeal with Blueberries and Almonds	10
Papaya and Spinach Green Smoothie	23
Peanut Butter and Banana Smoothie	16
Pineapple and Ginger Energizing Drink	26
Pistachio and Berry Crumble with Oat Topping	84
Poached Halibut with Caper and Lemon Sauce	59
Poached Pears in Red Wine with Cinnamon	82
Pomegranate and Blueberry Antioxidant Juice	25
Pork Tenderloin with Apple Cider Glaze	49
Pumpkin and Walnut Oat Bars with Spices	82
Quinoa and Avocado Salad with Lime Dressing	75
Quinoa and Black Bean Salad Cups	32
Quinoa and Black Bean Stuffed Bell Peppers	36
Quinoa and Black-Eyed Pea Salad	41

Quinoa Porridge with Chia Seeds and Banana	12
Red Lentil Soup with Turmeric and Cumin	39
Roasted Chickpeas with Herbs and Spices	27
Roasted Vegetable Salad with Balsamic Reduction	71
Seared Scallops with Spinach and Lemon	57
Seaweed Snacks with Sesame	33
Sliced Apple with Peanut Butter	31
Sliced Cucumber with Hummus Dip	28
Spicy Roasted Cauliflower Bites	33
Spicy Sriracha Shrimp with Brown Rice	60
Spinach and Cannellini Bean Spaghetti	39
Spinach and Mushroom Egg White Scramble	12
Spinach and Orange Salad with Candied Walnuts	75
Spinach and Strawberry Salad with Almonds	69
Sweet Potato and Black Bean Tacos	42
Sweet Potato and Kale Hash with Poached Eggs	14
Tandoori Spiced Trout with Mint Raita	61
Teriyaki Glazed Salmon with Steamed Asparagus	63
Three-Bean Chili with Tomatoes	40
Three-Bean Salad with Dijon Dressing	72
Tofu and Vegetable Breakfast Stir-Fry	13
Tofu and Vegetable Stir-Fry with Sesame	52
Trail Mix with Dark Chocolate and Almonds	33
Tuna Salad with Avocado Mayo	70
Turkey and Quinoa Stuffed Bell Peppers	54
Turkey and Vegetable Stir-Fry with Ginger	46
Turkey Burger with Avocado and Lettuce Wrap	47
Turkey Meatballs with Zucchini Noodles	51
Turmeric and Ginger Immune-Boosting Smoothie	21
Vegan Chia Seed Pudding with Berries	18
Veggie Omelette with Feta Cheese	16
Veggie Sticks with Tzatziki Sauce	31
Waldorf Salad with Greek Yogurt Dressing	74
Watermelon and Mint Cooler	25
Whole Grain Penne with Tomato and Basil	42
Whole Wheat Pancakes with Fresh Fruit Compote	13
Whole Wheat Spaghetti with Garlic and Broccoli	37

60 DAYS MEAL PLAN

Day	Breakfast	Lunch	Dinner	Dessert
1	Oatmeal with Blueberries and Almonds	Chickpea and Spinach Pasta	Barley and Mushroom Risotto	Baked Apples with Cinnamon and Walnuts
2	Greek Yogurt Parfait with Mixed Berries	Spinach and Cannellini Bean Spaghetti	Baked Cod with Tomato and Olive Relish	Frozen Banana Bites with Almond Butter and Dark Chocolate
3	Tofu and Vegetable Breakfast Stir-Fry	Three-Bean Chili with Tomatoes	Red Lentil Soup with Turmeric and Cumin	Almond and Date Energy Bites
4	Whole Wheat Pancakes with Fresh Fruit Compote	Ground Chicken Lettuce Wraps with Asian Sauce	Turkey Meatballs with Zucchini Noodles	Oatmeal Raisin Cookies with Oat Flour and Raisins
5	Cottage Cheese and Pineapple Breakfast Bowl	Chickpea and Spinach Pasta	Barley and Mushroom Risotto	Baked Apples with Cinnamon and Walnuts

6	Peanut Butter and Banana Smoothie	Spinach and Cannellini Bean Spaghetti	Baked Cod with Tomato and Olive Relish	Frozen Banana Bites with Almond Butter and Dark Chocolate
7	Vegan Chia Seed Pudding with Berries	Three-Bean Chili with Tomatoes	Red Lentil Soup with Turmeric and Cumin	Almond and Date Energy Bites
8	Buckwheat Pancakes with Raspberry Sauce	Ground Chicken Lettuce Wraps with Asian Sauce	Turkey Meatballs with Zucchini Noodles	Oatmeal Raisin Cookies with Oat Flour and Raisins
9	Sweet Potato and Kale Hash with Poached Eggs	Chickpea and Spinach Pasta	Barley and Mushroom Risotto	Baked Apples with Cinnamon and Walnuts
10	Broccoli and Tomato Breakfast Wrap	Spinach and Cannellini Bean Spaghetti	Baked Cod with Tomato and Olive Relish	Frozen Banana Bites with Almond Butter and Dark Chocolate
11	Avocado and Spinach Breakfast Burrito	Three-Bean Chili with Tomatoes	Red Lentil Soup with Turmeric and Cumin	Almond and Date Energy Bites
12	Oatmeal with Blueberries and Almonds	Ground Chicken Lettuce Wraps with Asian Sauce	Turkey Meatballs with Zucchini Noodles	Oatmeal Raisin Cookies with Oat Flour and Raisins

13	Greek Yogurt Parfait with Mixed Berries	Chickpea and Spinach Pasta	Barley and Mushroom Risotto	Baked Apples with Cinnamon and Walnuts
14	Tofu and Vegetable Breakfast Stir-Fry	Spinach and Cannellini Bean Spaghetti	Baked Cod with Tomato and Olive Relish	Frozen Banana Bites with Almond Butter and Dark Chocolate
15	Whole Wheat Pancakes with Fresh Fruit Compote	Three-Bean Chili with Tomatoes	Red Lentil Soup with Turmeric and Cumin	Almond and Date Energy Bites
16	Cottage Cheese and Pineapple Breakfast Bowl	Ground Chicken Lettuce Wraps with Asian Sauce	Turkey Meatballs with Zucchini Noodles	Oatmeal Raisin Cookies with Oat Flour and Raisins
17	Peanut Butter and Banana Smoothie	Chickpea and Spinach Pasta	Barley and Mushroom Risotto	Baked Apples with Cinnamon and Walnuts
18	Vegan Chia Seed Pudding with Berries	Spinach and Cannellini Bean Spaghetti	Baked Cod with Tomato and Olive Relish	Frozen Banana Bites with Almond Butter and Dark Chocolate
19	Broccoli and Tomato Breakfast Wrap	Three-Bean Chili with Tomatoes	Red Lentil Soup with Turmeric and Cumin	Almond and Date Energy Bites

20	Avocado and Spinach Breakfast Burrito	Ground Chicken Lettuce Wraps with Asian Sauce	Turkey Meatballs with Zucchini Noodles	Oatmeal Raisin Cookies with Oat Flour and Raisins
21	Oatmeal with Blueberries and Almonds	Chickpea and Spinach Pasta	Barley and Mushroom Risotto	Baked Apples with Cinnamon and Walnuts
22	Greek Yogurt Parfait with Mixed Berries	Spinach and Cannellini Bean Spaghetti	Baked Cod with Tomato and Olive Relish	Frozen Banana Bites with Almond Butter and Dark Chocolate
23	Tofu and Vegetable Breakfast Stir-Fry	Three-Bean Chili with Tomatoes	Red Lentil Soup with Turmeric and Cumin	Almond and Date Energy Bites
24	Whole Wheat Pancakes with Fresh Fruit Compote	Ground Chicken Lettuce Wraps with Asian Sauce	Turkey Meatballs with Zucchini Noodles	Oatmeal Raisin Cookies with Oat Flour and Raisins
25	Cottage Cheese and Pineapple Breakfast Bowl	Chickpea and Spinach Pasta	Barley and Mushroom Risotto	Baked Apples with Cinnamon and Walnuts
26	Peanut Butter and Banana Smoothie	Spinach and Cannellini Bean Spaghetti	Baked Cod with Tomato and Olive Relish	Frozen Banana Bites with Almond Butter and Dark Chocolate

27	Vegan Chia Seed Pudding with Berries	Three-Bean Chili with Tomatoes	Red Lentil Soup with Turmeric and Cumin	Almond and Date Energy Bites
28	Broccoli and Tomato Breakfast Wrap	Ground Chicken Lettuce Wraps with Asian Sauce	Turkey Meatballs with Zucchini Noodles	Oatmeal Raisin Cookies with Oat Flour and Raisins
29	Avocado and Spinach Breakfast Burrito	Chickpea and Spinach Pasta	Barley and Mushroom Risotto	Baked Apples with Cinnamon and Walnuts
30	Oatmeal with Blueberries and Almonds	Spinach and Cannellini Bean Spaghetti	Baked Cod with Tomato and Olive Relish	Frozen Banana Bites with Almond Butter and Dark Chocolate
31	Greek Yogurt Parfait with Mixed Berries	Three-Bean Chili with Tomatoes	Red Lentil Soup with Turmeric and Cumin	Almond and Date Energy Bites
32	Tofu and Vegetable Breakfast Stir-Fry	Ground Chicken Lettuce Wraps with Asian Sauce	Turkey Meatballs with Zucchini Noodles	Oatmeal Raisin Cookies with Oat Flour and Raisins
33	Whole Wheat Pancakes with Fresh Fruit Compote	Chickpea and Spinach Pasta	Barley and Mushroom Risotto	Baked Apples with Cinnamon and Walnuts

34	Cottage Cheese and Pineapple Breakfast Bowl	Spinach and Cannellini Bean Spaghetti	Baked Cod with Tomato and Olive Relish	Frozen Banana Bites with Almond Butter and Dark Chocolate
35	Peanut Butter and Banana Smoothie	Three-Bean Chili with Tomatoes	Red Lentil Soup with Turmeric and Cumin	Almond and Date Energy Bites
36	Vegan Chia Seed Pudding with Berries	Ground Chicken Lettuce Wraps with Asian Sauce	Turkey Meatballs with Zucchini Noodles	Oatmeal Raisin Cookies with Oat Flour and Raisins
37	Broccoli and Tomato Breakfast Wrap	Chickpea and Spinach Pasta	Barley and Mushroom Risotto	Baked Apples with Cinnamon and Walnuts
38	Avocado and Spinach Breakfast Burrito	Spinach and Cannellini Bean Spaghetti	Baked Cod with Tomato and Olive Relish	Frozen Banana Bites with Almond Butter and Dark Chocolate
39	Oatmeal with Blueberries and Almonds	Three-Bean Chili with Tomatoes	Red Lentil Soup with Turmeric and Cumin	Almond and Date Energy Bites
40	Greek Yogurt Parfait with Mixed Berries	Ground Chicken Lettuce Wraps with Asian Sauce	Turkey Meatballs with Zucchini Noodles	Oatmeal Raisin Cookies with Oat Flour and Raisins

41	Tofu and Vegetable Breakfast Stir-Fry	Chickpea and Spinach Pasta	Barley and Mushroom Risotto	Baked Apples with Cinnamon and Walnuts
42	Whole Wheat Pancakes with Fresh Fruit Compote	Spinach and Cannellini Bean Spaghetti	Baked Cod with Tomato and Olive Relish	Frozen Banana Bites with Almond Butter and Dark Chocolate
43	Cottage Cheese and Pineapple Breakfast Bowl	Three-Bean Chili with Tomatoes	Red Lentil Soup with Turmeric and Cumin	Almond and Date Energy Bites
44	Peanut Butter and Banana Smoothie	Ground Chicken Lettuce Wraps with Asian Sauce	Turkey Meatballs with Zucchini Noodles	Oatmeal Raisin Cookies with Oat Flour and Raisins
45	Vegan Chia Seed Pudding with Berries	Chickpea and Spinach Pasta	Barley and Mushroom Risotto	Baked Apples with Cinnamon and Walnuts
46	Broccoli and Tomato Breakfast Wrap	Spinach and Cannellini Bean Spaghetti	Baked Cod with Tomato and Olive Relish	Frozen Banana Bites with Almond Butter and Dark Chocolate
47	Avocado and Spinach Breakfast Burrito	Three-Bean Chili with Tomatoes	Red Lentil Soup with Turmeric and Cumin	Almond and Date Energy Bites

48	Oatmeal with Blueberries and Almonds	Ground Chicken Lettuce Wraps with Asian Sauce	Turkey Meatballs with Zucchini Noodles	Oatmeal Raisin Cookies with Oat Flour and Raisins
49	Greek Yogurt Parfait with Mixed Berries	Chickpea and Spinach Pasta	Barley and Mushroom Risotto	Baked Apples with Cinnamon and Walnuts
50	Tofu and Vegetable Breakfast Stir-Fry	Spinach and Cannellini Bean Spaghetti	Baked Cod with Tomato and Olive Relish	Frozen Banana Bites with Almond Butter and Dark Chocolate
51	Whole Wheat Pancakes with Fresh Fruit Compote	Three-Bean Chili with Tomatoes	Red Lentil Soup with Turmeric and Cumin	Almond and Date Energy Bites
52	Cottage Cheese and Pineapple Breakfast Bowl	Ground Chicken Lettuce Wraps with Asian Sauce	Turkey Meatballs with Zucchini Noodles	Oatmeal Raisin Cookies with Oat Flour and Raisins
53	Peanut Butter and Banana Smoothie	Chickpea and Spinach Pasta	Barley and Mushroom Risotto	Baked Apples with Cinnamon and Walnuts
54	Vegan Chia Seed Pudding with Berries	Spinach and Cannellini Bean Spaghetti	Baked Cod with Tomato and Olive Relish	Frozen Banana Bites with Almond Butter and Dark Chocolate

55	Broccoli and Tomato Breakfast Wrap	Three-Bean Chili with Tomatoes	Red Lentil Soup with Turmeric and Cumin	Almond and Date Energy Bites
56	Avocado and Spinach Breakfast Burrito	Ground Chicken Lettuce Wraps with Asian Sauce	Turkey Meatballs with Zucchini Noodles	Oatmeal Raisin Cookies with Oat Flour and Raisins
57	Oatmeal with Blueberries and Almonds	Chickpea and Spinach Pasta	Barley and Mushroom Risotto	Baked Apples with Cinnamon and Walnuts
58	Greek Yogurt Parfait with Mixed Berries	Spinach and Cannellini Bean Spaghetti	Baked Cod with Tomato and Olive Relish	Frozen Banana Bites with Almond Butter and Dark Chocolate
59	Tofu and Vegetable Breakfast Stir-Fry	Three-Bean Chili with Tomatoes	Red Lentil Soup with Turmeric and Cumin	Almond and Date Energy Bites
60	Whole Wheat Pancakes with Fresh Fruit Compote	Ground Chicken Lettuce Wraps with Asian Sauce	Turkey Meatballs with Zucchini Noodles	Oatmeal Raisin Cookies with Oat Flour and Raisins

Kitchen Measurement Abbreviations (Standard and Metric)

Abbreviation	Measurement
tbsp	tablespoon
tsp	teaspoon
oz	ounce
fl. oz	fluid ounce
c	cup
qt	quart
pt	pint
gal	gallon
lb	pound
mL	milliliter
g	grams
kg	kilogram
l	liter

Dry Measurements Conversion Chart

Teaspoons	Tablespoons	Cups
3 tsp	1 tbsp	1/16 c
6 tsp	2 tbsp	1/8 c
12 tsp	4 tbsp	1/4 c
24 tsp	8 tbsp	1/2 c
36 tsp	12 tbsp	3/4 c
48 tsp	16 tbsp	1 c

Liquid Measurements Conversion Chart

Fluid Ounces	Cups	Pints	Quarts	Gallons
8 fl. oz	1 c	1/2 pt	1/4 qt	1/16 gal
16 fl. oz	2 c	1 pt	1/2 qt	1/8 gal
32 fl. oz	4 c	2 pt	1 qt	1/4 gal
64 fl. oz	8 c	4 pt	2 qt	1/2 gal
128 fl. oz	16 c	8 pt	4 qt	1 gal

Butter Measurements Chart

Sticks	Cups	Tablespoons	Ounces	Grams
1/2 stick	1/4 c	4 tbsp	2 oz	57.5 g
1 stick	1/2 c	8 tbsp	4 oz	115 g
2 sticks	1 c	16 tbsp	8 oz	230 g

Oven Temperatures Conversion

(Degrees) Celsius	(Degrees) Fahrenheit
120 C	250 F
160 C	320 F
180 C	350 F
205 C	400 F
220 C	425 F

Weight Equivalents US Standard Metric (approximate)

½ ounce	15 g
1 ounce	30 g
2 ounces	60 g
4 ounces	115 g
8 ounces	225 g
12 ounces	340 g

Take Your Gift Now!

SCAN ME!

Printed in Great Britain
by Amazon

44213893R00057